JANET MORLEY

All Desires Known

Third Edition

Morehouse Publishing

NEW YORK · HARRISBURG · DENVER

This revised edition first published in Great Britain in 2005 by Society for Promoting Christian Knowledge (SPCK), 36 Causton Street, London, SW1P 4ST.

American edition published by
Morehouse Publishing, P.O. Box 1321, Harrisburg, PA 17105
Morehouse Publishing, 445 Fifth Avenue, New York, NY 10016
Morehouse Publishing is an imprint of Church Publishing Incorporated.

Cover design by Corey Kent

Library of Congress Cataloging-in-Publication Data

Morley, Janet.
  All desires known / Janet Morley.— 3rd ed.
    p. cm.
  Includes bibliographical references and index.
  ISBN-13: 978-0-8192-2225-1 (pbk.)
  1. Episcopal Church—Prayer-books and devotions—English. 2.
Episcopal Church—Liturgy. 3. Church of England—Prayer-books and
devotions—English. 4. Church of England—Liturgy. 5. Nonsexist
language—Religious aspects—Episcopal Church. 6. Anglican
Communion—Prayer-books and devotions—English. 7. Anglican
Communion—Liturgy. 8. God—Fatherhood. I. Title.
  BX5947.N64M67 2006
  264'.036—dc22
                                    2005032436

Contents

Preface

'All desires known': this phrase has always evoked in me that distinctive stance which I associate with authentic worship: namely, an appalled sense of self-exposure combined with a curious but profound relief; and so to write under this title has been both a discipline and a comfort. I have chosen it because I understand the Christian life to be about the integration of desire: our personal desires, our political vision, and our longing for God. So far from being separate or in competition with one another, I believe that our deepest desires ultimately spring from the same source; and worship is the place where this can be acknowledged.

I have also tried, in my writing, to integrate my faith and my feminism. For me, as for many others in recent years, the women's movement has been the place where my Christian faith has been most strongly challenged, and yet has also been the most important resource for its renewed growth and energy. At the same time, the persistently subversive character of the gospel operates to prevent the feminist struggle for the empowerment of women from turning into one more ideology of self-justification.

In worship, our ideologies stand exposed, and nowhere is this clearer than in the assumptions expressed in our language. Increasingly, the convention by which God has been addressed in terms that are exclusively male has caused discomfort among worshippers; but the problem of finding new words is not simple. There is often something unsatisfactory about altering existing texts to make them 'sound'. In any case, the effort to erase gender from our image of God, or to make everything fair and balanced, can produce linguistic awkwardness and tend towards a neutrality in prayer which I think is inappropriate. Much more potentially creative is the writing of new texts in vigorous language, which also respects and inhabits ancient worship forms, evocative biblical imagery, and familiar cadences and rhythms.

'Inclusive language' does not have to mean replacing 'Almighty Father' with an (equally problematic) 'Almighty Mother'. I have found that to examine how and why the feminine has been omitted from our ways of addressing God is to discover also what else has been left out. To release ourselves from the habit of always using certain predictable (and perhaps scarcely-noticed) formulae for the beginning of a prayer, may free the imagination to explore the unimaginable ways in which God reaches us. At the same time, the very range of possible imagery forbids us to *identify* God with any limited form of words. We have a model for this practice in the Hebrew psalms, and in the long but often submerged tradition of Christian mysticism. In both, we find not only a wealth of exuberant but provisional imagery, but also a distinctive blend of the passionate and the political, that can express the integration of our desire.

In some of my prayers I do use explicitly feminine imagery for God. This is not because I seek to worship a 'goddess' – any more than generations of calling God 'He' implies belief in a literally male 'god'. It is that I have come to acknowledge how profoundly the women friends whom I love and struggle with have helped me to articulate my longings, and have mediated the love of God to me. But I also recognize that if, as women, our only access to the *strangeness* of God is through the 'otherness' of the male image, then that will insist on the wrong kind of otherness; and it may encourage us to avoid some of the more painful and intimate dilemmas of religious belief. Feminine imagery not only affirms a comfortable closeness for women to the God in whose image we are made: it also prevents us from distancing ourselves – as we can do with 'male' language – from the uncomfortable, even frightening closeness of the difficult God who is not made in our image.

The collects

Of all the prayers in *All Desires Known*, the section of collects has turned out to be the most frequently used across the Churches, since they were first published. At that time the Church of England followed a two-year lectionary, which was incorporated in the *Alternative Service Book 1980* (ASB), and the collects in *All Desires Known* followed the themes set in the ASB across the Church's year. Since then a majority of the Churches have agreed to follow the three-year *Revised Common Lectionary.* The Church of England's *Common Worship Lectionary* is a version of this. The collects here are therefore arranged and indexed on a new system, in order to enable the reader to find a suitable collect on a particular Sunday. Since the collects in this book are strongly related to biblical passages and themes, they have been given thematic titles for ease of reference, and the Sundays in which relevant passages may be read are indicated below each collect. There is also an index based on the *Common Worship* sequence of biblical passages, and an index based on biblical order. Occasional new collects have been added.

The formal prayers

These are written in various traditional forms: litany, canticle, eucharistic prayer, confession, blessing. Some are linked to specific or festival use; others will be adaptable to a range of settings. Some are more suitable for women's groups; others presuppose a mixed congregation. Very many were written initially for a particular occasion of use by a worshipping group, and I have indicated this as appropriate. Theologically, it will be noted that I frequently refer to the Wisdom of God, who is personified in feminine terms in an important strand of Jewish thought. Strong and significant echoes of the Wisdom tradition in fact underlie many of the crucial Christological passages of the New Testament. The eucharistic prayers in this section aim to combine traditional Christian theology of the eucharist with a special emphasis on, and celebration for, the witness of women in the life of Jesus.

The psalms and poems

The genre of psalm is particularly interesting from a feminist point of view, since it allows for an intense individuality of utterance which, because of how psalms have always been used, can nevertheless convey a communal voice. Hence it is an excellent form for expressing the perception that the personal is political; and the ancient heritage of the psalm carries considerable authority of tone.

However, because of the (still unusual) feminine language for God, and because of the intimacy of the material in this section, I recommend that the psalms and poems should only be introduced into group worship if careful thought has been given about their appropriateness. Women can feel peculiarly exposed by this language, and may understandably resent its being imposed without preparation. It is valuable to include opportunity for discussion, where mixed feelings can be explored.

'Thy Kingdom Come'

This section of new material is taken from a range of liturgical material that I wrote while I was employed by Christian Aid (1988–1999). Some of the prayers appeared in anthologies, but many were produced for ephemeral occasions such as Christian Aid Week services, or Harvest celebrations. They have been selected for their coherence with the concept of this book, and are reproduced by kind permission of Christian Aid, with whom I share the copyright in this material.

Working for Christian Aid was a hugely important perspective from which to write prayers and liturgies. I found that my feminism was challenged to stretch, as I encountered the critique of global systems of injustice from which I benefited as a Western woman. My prayers needed to reflect the urgent concerns of the poorest people in our world, but considered from the perspective of living in the developed world. Whether our own circumstances are wealth or relative poverty, we cannot escape being part of a global market that consumes natural resources prodigiously, keeps poorer nations endlessly indebted, and forces down the price of raw goods at the expense of those who labour to produce them.

It is painful to be part of a world that is full of violence and injustice, and even when we are shielded from some kinds of suffering, we need to pray for ourselves as well as for those who bear the heaviest burdens. The Lord's Prayer, at the heart of the Christian tradition, offers us a model of prayer which is built on the hope of a world in which God's name will be honoured, and all will be freed from the grip of hunger, evil and debt.

Prayer for the world involves daring to keep our eyes open, refusing to distance ourselves from what is painful to contemplate; it involves noticing and celebrating difference. In it, we seek to articulate our desire to be fully human in a world which is not yet as God intended it to be, and to commit ourselves to working with others to enable God's will to be done. The introduction I wrote to *Dear Life*, from which some of the additional material has been selected, puts it thus:

> So far from being a passive or soft option, prayer underpins the other responses we make to the world. If we pray honestly and with open hearts, we shall not be able to escape the questions about how we personally apportion our money, or whether we are actually using our influence to bring about change. But prayer also protects us – from the illusion that we can change things entirely under our own power, and from the burnout that comes from believing that we must. When we pray, we are asking to place ourselves and those for whom we pray together under the power of God; and we know that we are not alone . . .
>
> Praying for the world is a strong activity; it is work for grownups, for those of us who are not afraid to risk knowing about our own helplessness and mortality, as well as our strengths, or to contemplate steadily the evils in which we are all involved. It is for those who have decided to choose hope, in a world where despair has, on the surface, the more convincing arguments. It is for those who want to celebrate our connectedness with sisters and brothers across the world.

Janet Morley 1988, revised 2005

Collects

Collects

1. ANNUNCIATION/NOT AMONG THE IMPRESSIVE

O unknown God,
whose presence is announced
not among the impressive
but in obscurity:
come, overshadow us now,
and speak to our hidden places;
that, entering your darkness with joy,
we may choose to co-operate with you,
through Jesus Christ, **Amen.**

> Luke 1.2–38; 1 Corinthians 1.26–end
> *Advent 4 (BC); Proper 6 (BC); Annunciation (ABC)*

2. APPALLING SACRIFICE

Fearful God,
you require of our love
appalling sacrifice;
and your lasting promise
is contained in contradiction.
May we so lay on your altar
our dearest desires
that we may receive them back from you
as unaccountable gift,
through Jesus Christ, **Amen.**

> Genesis 22.1–18; Mark 8.34–35
> *Lent 2 (B); Proper 8 (ABC); Proper 19 (B)*

3. A SCANDAL TO MANY

Christ our cornerstone,
you were recognized at your presentation
as a sign of hope for the world,
but also as a stumbling-block for many:
may we so present our bodies to your service,
that, in sharing your scandal,
we may become a people acceptable to you,
in your name, **Amen.**

Luke 2.22–35; 1 Peter 2.1–10
Christmas 1 (B); Epiphany 4 (C); Presentation (ABC)

4. A STRANGE LAND

O God, whom to follow
is to risk our whole lives:
as Ruth and Naomi
loved and held to one another,
abandoning the ways of the past,
so may we also not be divided,
but travel together
into that strange land where you will lead us
through Jesus Christ, **Amen.**

Ruth 1.8–17
4 before Advent (B)
[Revised Common Lectionary]

5. BEARING CHRIST IN OUR BODY

O Christ,
to serve whose gospel you have filled us
not with timidity, but power:
help us bear in our body
your wounded humanity;
that we may bodily show forth
your resurrection life, **Amen.**

4

John 5.1–9; 2 Corinthians 4.1–12; 2 Timothy 1.7
Easter 6 (C); Proper 4 (B); Proper 22 (C); Saints' Days

6. CALL/SAINTS

Christ, whose insistent call
disturbs our settled lives:
give us discernment to hear your word,
grace to relinquish our tasks,
and courage to follow empty-handed
wherever you may lead;
that the voice of your gospel
may reach to the ends of the earth, **Amen.**

Matthew 4.12–20; Romans 10.12–18
Epiphany 2 (AB); Epiphany 3 (A); Proper 1 (C); Saints' Days

7. CALLED TO THE FEAST

O God, at whose table
we are no longer strangers;
may we not refuse your call
through pride or fear,
but approach with confidence
to find our home in you
through Jesus Christ, **Amen.**

Matthew 22.1–14; Acts 2.37–41; Ephesians 2.19–20; 1 Peter 2.1–10
*Easter 3 (A); Easter 5 (ABC); Proper 17 (C); Proper 23 (A); Saints'
Days; Thomas; Dedication*

8. CHOOSE LIFE

God of crisis,
you lay before us
either blessing or curse.
In our confusion
give us clarity;
and in our hesitation
the courage to choose boldly
the way that leads to you,
through Jesus Christ, **Amen.**

Deuteronomy 11.18–28; 30.15–20; 1 John 2.22–end
Proper 2 (A); Proper 4 (A); Proper 18 (C);
2 before Advent (A)

9. CHRIST OUR BROTHER

Christ our brother,
in you there is neither Jew nor Gentile,
neither male nor female;
yet you received the mark of the covenant
and took upon you
the precious burden of the law.
May we so accept in our bodies
our own particular struggle and promise,
that we also may break down barriers
in your name, **Amen.**

Luke 2.15–21; Galatians 3.28
Christmas 1 (B); Proper 7 (C); Holy Name (ABC);
Birth of John the Baptist (ABC)

10. CLOUD OF UNKNOWING

O God,
you withdraw from our sight
that you may be known by our love:
help us to enter the cloud
where you are hidden,
and surrender all our certainty
to the darkness of faith
in Jesus Christ, **Amen.**

Acts 1.1–11
Ascension Day (ABC)

11. COST OF DISCIPLESHIP/ WAY OF THE CROSS

Jesus our brother,
you followed the necessary path
and were broken on our behalf.
May we neither cling to our pain
where it is futile,
nor refuse to embrace the cost
when it is required of us:
that in losing our selves for your sake,
we may be brought to new life, **Amen.**

Matthew 16.13–end; Mark 8.27–end; Luke 9.18–27
Lent 2 (B); Palm Sunday (C); Proper 17 (A); Proper 19 (B)

12. COURAGE TO PROCLAIM YOU

O God unknown,
in our mother's womb
you formed us for your glory.
Give us a heart to long for you,
grace to discern you,
and courage to proclaim you;
through the one whom you loved
before the foundation of the world,
our saviour Jesus Christ, **Amen.**

Isaiah 49.1–6; Jeremiah 1.4–10; John 17.20–end; Acts 17.22–end
*Epiphany 2 (AB); Lent 4 (AB); Tuesday in Holy Week (ABC); Easter 6
(AB); Easter 7 (C); Proper 16 (C); Conversion of Paul; Saints' Days*

13. CREATION/INSPIRATION

Holy Spirit,
mighty wind of God,
inhabit our darkness
brood over our abyss
and speak to our chaos;
that we may breathe with your life
and share your creation
in the power of Jesus Christ, **Amen.**

Genesis 1 and 2; John 1.29–42
*Baptism of Christ (ABC); Epiphany 2 (A); 2 before Lent (A);
Lent 5 (AB)*

14. DEFENDER OF THE HELPLESS

God of the dispossessed,
defender of the helpless,
you grieve with all the ~~women~~ who weep
because their children are no more:
may we also ~~refuse to be comforted~~ *grieve with you*
until the violence of the strong
has been confounded,
and the broken victims have been set free
in the name of Jesus Christ, **Amen.**

Matthew 2.13–18; 1 Corinthians 1.2–9
Christmas 1 (A); Holy Innocents (ABC)

15. DEPENDENCE ON GOD'S WORD

God of all trust,
may we who confess your faith
prove it in our lives,
with abundant joy,
outrageous hope
and dependence on nothing
but your word alone,
through Jesus Christ, **Amen.**

Jeremiah 32.6–15; Luke 7.1–10
Sunday next before Lent (C); Proper 4 (C); Proper 21 (C)

16. DESERT CHOICES

Spirit of integrity,
you drive us into the desert
to search out our truth.
Give us clarity to know what is right,
and courage to reject what is expedient;
that we may abandon the false innocence
of failing to choose at all,
but may follow the purposes of Jesus Christ, **Amen.**

Matthew 4.1–11; Mark 1.9–15; Luke 4.1–13
Lent 1 (ABC)

17. DISTURB THE RIGHTEOUS

Christ our companion,
you came not to humiliate the sinner
but to disturb the righteous.
Welcome us when we are put to shame, ·
but challenge our smugness,
that we may truly turn from what is evil,
and be freed even from our virtues,
in your name, **Amen.**

Mark 2.3–17; John 8.2–11
Proper 3 (B); Ash Wednesday (ABC); Proper 19 (AC); Proper 25 (C)

18. EASTER – FORGIVENESS

Christ our friend,
you ask for our love
in spite of our betrayal.
Give us courage to embrace forgiveness,
know you again,
and trust ourselves in you, **Amen.**

John 21.1–19
Wednesday in Holy Week (ABC); Easter 3 (C)

19. EASTER – IN TIME OF GRIEF

O God,
you call us to commitment
even at the point of despair.
Give us the faith of Martha
to find in our anger and loss
a truthful place to proclaim you
our resurrection and life,
through Jesus Christ, **Amen.**

John 11.17–27
Lent 5 (A)

20. EASTER – MARY MAGDALENE

Christ our healer,
beloved and remembered by women:
speak to the grief which makes us forget,
and the terror that makes us cling,
and give us back our name;
that we may greet you clearly,
and proclaim your risen life, **Amen.**

John 20.11–18
Easter Day (ABC); Mary Magdalene

21. EASTER – OPEN OUR GRAVES

God of terror and joy,
you arise to shake the earth.
Open our graves
and give us back the past;
so that all that has been buried
may be freed and forgiven,
and our lives may return to you
through the risen Christ, **Amen.**

Isaiah 2.19–21; Matthew 27.51–54; 28.1–10; Mark 16.1–8;
John 11.32–34
*Lent 5 (AB); Palm Sunday (A); Easter Vigil (ABC);
Easter Day (ABC); All Saints' Day (B)*

22. EASTER – PRESENCE OF CHRIST

Risen Christ,
whose absence leaves us paralysed,
but whose presence is overwhelming:
breathe on us
with your abundant life;
that where we cannot see
we may have courage to believe
that we may be raised with you, **Amen.**

John 20.19–31
Easter 2 (ABC); Easter 3 (B); Thomas

23. EASTER – RECOGNITION

O unfamiliar God,
we seek you in the places
you have already left,
and fail to see you
even when you stand before us.
Grant us so to recognize your strangeness
that we need not cling to our familiar grief,
but may be freed to proclaim resurrection
in the name of Christ, **Amen.**

John 20.1–18
Easter Day (ABC); Mary Magdalene

24. EASTER – ROAD TO EMMAUS

O God whose greeting we miss
and whose departure we delay:
make our hearts burn with insight
on our ordinary road;
that, as we grasp you in the broken bread,
we may also let you go,
and return to speak your word of life
in the name of Christ, **Amen.**

Luke 24.13–48
Easter 3 (AB)

25. EASTER – WITNESS OF THE WOMEN

O God, the power of the powerless,
you have chosen as your witnesses
those whose voice is not heard.
Grant that, as women first announced
the resurrection
though they were not believed,
we too may have courage
to persist in proclaiming your word,
in the power of Jesus Christ, **Amen.**

Luke 24.1–11
Easter Day (C)

26. EPIPHANY/REVELATION

O God, the source of all insight,
whose coming was revealed to the nations
not among men of power
but on a woman's lap:
give us grace to seek you
where you may be found,
that the wisdom of this world may be humbled
and discover your unexpected joy,
through Jesus Christ, **Amen.**

Matthew 2.1–12
Epiphany of the Lord (ABC)

27. EUCHARIST

O God who took human flesh
that you might be intimate with us:
may we so taste and touch you
in our bodily life
that we may discern and celebrate
your body in the world,
through Jesus Christ, **Amen.**

John 6.51–58; 1 Corinthians 11.23–29
Maundy Thursday (ABC); Proper 15 (B); Corpus Christi

13

28. FALL/ACCUSING EACH OTHER

Holy God,
we are born into a world
tissued and structured by sin.
When we proclaim our innocence
and seek to accuse each other,
give us the grace to know that we are naked;
that we may cry out to you alone
through Jesus Christ, **Amen.**

Genesis 3.1–15; 1 John 1.5–10
Lent 1 (A); Proper 5 (AB); Proper 13 (B); Proper 22 (AB)

29. FILLED WITH LONGING

Vulnerable God,
you challenge the powers that rule this world
through the needy, the compassionate,
and those who are filled with longing.
Make us hunger and thirst to see right prevail,
and single-minded in seeking peace;
that we may see your face
and be satisfied in you,
through Jesus Christ, **Amen.**

Matthew 5.1–12; 1 Corinthians 2.1–10; 4.8–13
*Epiphany 4 (A); Proper 2 (C); Lent 3 (C); All Saints' Day (ABC);
Saints' Days*

30. GIVING BIRTH TO CHANGE

O God for whom we long
as a woman in labour
longs for her delivery:
give us courage to wait,
strength to push,
and discernment to know the right time;
that we may bring into the world
your joyful peace,
through Jesus Christ, **Amen.**

John 16.12–24; Romans 8.12–25
2 before Lent (A); Proper 11 (A)

31. GOD OF COMMUNITY

God of community,
whose call is more insistent
than ties of family or blood:
may we so respect and love
those whose lives are linked with ours
that we fail not in loyalty to you,
but make choices according to your will,
through Jesus Christ, **Amen.**

Mark 3.31–end; Luke 2.41–end
Christmas 1 (C); Proper 5 (B)

32. GOD OF THE POOR

God of the poor,
we long to meet you
yet always miss you;
we strive to help you,
yet only discover our need.
Interrupt our comfort
with your nakedness,
touch our possessiveness
with your poverty,
and surprise our guilt
with the grace of your welcome
in Jesus Christ. **Amen.**

Matthew 25.31–46; Mark 10.17–31
Proper 23 (B); Christ the King (A)

33. GOD OUR DESIRE

God our desire,
whose coming we look for,
but whose arrival is unexpected:
here in the darkness
make us urgent to greet you,
and open yourself to our longing
that we may be known by you
through Jesus Christ, **Amen.**

Matthew 25.1–13
Proper 9 (A); Proper 17 (B); 3 before Advent (A)

34. GOD'S FRUITFUL WORD

O God our disturber,
whose speech is pregnant with power
and whose word will be fulfilled:
may we know ourselves unsatisfied
with all that distorts your truth,
and make our hearts attentive
to your liberating voice,
in Jesus Christ, **Amen.**

Isaiah 55.1–11; Luke 1.46b–55; Luke 4.14–21; 2 Timothy 3.14—4.5
*Advent 3 (ABC); Epiphany 3 (C); Easter Vigil (ABC); Easter 6 (B);
Proper 3 (B); Proper 10 (AC); Proper 24 (C); Bible Sunday (BC)*

35. GOD'S UNCONTAINABLE WORD

God of truth and terror,
whose word we can with comfort
neither speak nor contain;
give us courage to release the fire
you have shut up in our bones,
and strength in your spirit
to withstand the burning,
through Jesus Christ, **Amen.**

Jeremiah 20.7–11; Matthew 10.16–22
Proper 7 (ABC); 3 before Advent (B); Saints' Days

36. GOOD FRIDAY – PASSION

O God, the source of our passion,
who took upon you our unprotected flesh,
kindle in us
your anger and desire;
that in suffering we may not be consumed,
but hold fast to you
through Jesus Christ, **Amen.**

Hebrews 4.14–16; 5.7–9
Good Friday (ABC)

37. GOOD FRIDAY – SUFFERING SERVANT

Christ our victim,
whose beauty was disfigured
and whose body torn upon the cross;
open wide your arms
to embrace our tortured world,
that we may not turn away our eyes,
but abandon ourselves to your mercy, **Amen.**

Isaiah 52.13–end; John 18.1—19.37
Good Friday (ABC)

38. GOOD FRIDAY – WITNESS OF THE WOMEN

Christ, whose bitter agony
was watched from afar by women:
enable us to follow the example
of their persistent love;
that, being steadfast in the face of horror,
we may also know the place of resurrection,
in your name, **Amen.**

Mark 15.4—16.1
Good Friday (ABC); Easter Vigil (B)

39. HOLY RAGE

Righteous God,
you plead the cause
of the poor and unprotected.
Fill us with holy rage
when justice is delayed,
and give us the persistence
to require those rights that are denied;
for your name's sake, **Amen.**

Luke 18.1–8
Proper 14 (C); Proper 22 (B); Proper 24 (C)

40. I AM WHO I AM

God whose holy name
defies our definition,
but whose will is known
in freeing the oppressed:
make us to be one
with all who cry for justice;
that we who speak your praise
may struggle for your truth,
through Jesus Christ, **Amen.**

Exodus 3.7–15
Proper 16 (ABC); Proper 17 (A)

41. INCARNATION – FULLNESS OF GLORY

Loving Word of God,
you have shown us the fullness of your glory
in taking human flesh.
Fill us, in our bodily life,
with your grace and truth;
that our pleasure may be boundless,
and our integrity complete,
in your name, **Amen.**

John 1.14–18
Christmas 2 (ABC)

42. INCARNATION – WORD MADE FLESH

God our beloved,
born of a woman's body,
you came that we might look upon you,
and handle you with our own hands.
May we so cherish one another in our bodies
that we may also be touched by you;
through the Word made flesh, Jesus Christ, **Amen.**

John 1.1–14; 1 John 1.1–4
Christmas Eve/Christmas Day (ABC)

43. INTIMACY AND CHALLENGE

God of intimacy,
you surround us with friends and family
to cherish and to challenge.
May we so give and receive caring
in the details of our lives
that we also remain faithful
to your greater demands,
through Jesus Christ, **Amen.**

Mark 3.20–35; Luke 11.1–13
Proper 5 (B); Proper 12 (C)

44. JOY BEYOND MEASURE

O God of celebration,
you have kept the good wine until now –
the wine that we have longed for,
but never thought to taste.
Take the tapwater of our lives –
our struggles and our dullness –
and with your grace
make strong and dark and joyful
all that our hearts contain,
through Jesus Christ our Lord, **Amen.**

John 2.1–11
Epiphany 2 (C); Epiphany 3 (B); Epiphany 4 (A)

45. JUSTIFIED BY FAITH ALONE

O God, before whose face
we are not made righteous
even by being right:
free us from the need
to justify ourselves
by our own anxious striving,
that we may be abandoned
to faith in you alone,
through Jesus Christ, **Amen.**

Matthew 6.24–end; Romans 5.1–11
2 before Lent (A); Lent 3 (A); Trinity Sunday (C); Proper 6 (A)

46. KNOWING OUR NEED

O Christ for whom we search,
our help when help has failed:
give us courage to expose our need
and ask to be made whole;
that, being touched by you,
we may be raised to new life
in the power of your name, **Amen.**

Matthew 9.18–26; Mark 5.21–43
Proper 5 (A); Proper 8 (B)

47. LABOUR PANGS OF THE NEW AGE

God our deliverer,
whose approaching birth
still shakes the foundations of our world:
may we so wait for your coming
with eagerness and hope
that we embrace without terror
the labour pangs of the new age,
through Jesus Christ, **Amen.**

> Mark 13.8–end; Luke 21.25–36; Romans 8.18–25;
> 1 Thessalonians 5.1–11
> *Advent 1 (ABC); 2 before Lent (A); Pentecost (ABC); Proper 11 (A);*
> *2 before Advent (ABC); Saints' Days*

48. LETTING GO

Christ our lover
to whom we try to cling:
as you have reached into our depths
and drawn us to love you,
so make us open, freely to let you go;
that you may return in unexpected power
to change the world through us,
in your name, **Amen.**

> Luke 24.45–end
> *Ascension Day (ABC); Easter 7 (ABC)*

49. LOVE YOUR ENEMIES

Christ our teacher,
you urge us beyond all reason
to love our enemies,
and pray for our oppressors.
May we embrace such folly
not through subservience, but strength;
that unmeasured generosity
may be poured into our lap,
through Jesus Christ, **Amen.**

Matthew 5.39–44; Luke 6.27–38
Proper 3 (AC)

50. MARY'S ASSENT

O God,
you fulfil our desire
beyond what we can bear:
as Mary gave her appalled assent
to your intimate promise,
so may we open ourselves also
to contain your life within us,
through Jesus Christ, **Amen.**

Luke 1.2–38
Advent 4 (BC); Annunciation (ABC)

51. MOST HOLY AND MOST HUMBLE

Mighty God,
most holy and most humble,
you have chosen to hear our cry
and share our poverty.
Come close to our world,
kindle our hearts
and melt our despair,
that with all your creatures
we may live in hope;
through Jesus Christ our King, **Amen.**

John 1.1–14
*Christmas Day (ABC); 2 before Lent (B); Lent 4 (B);
Christ the King (C)*

52. MOTHERLY GOD

God our mother,
you hold our life within you,
nourish us at your breast,
and teach us to walk alone.
Help us so to receive your tenderness
and respond to your challenge
that others may draw life from us,
in your name, **Amen.**

Isaiah 46.3–4; 49.14–16; 66.7–13; Hosea 11.1–4
Mothering Sunday (ABC)

53. MOTHERLY SAVIOUR

Christ our true mother,
you have carried us within you,
laboured with us,
and brought us forth to bliss.
Enclose us in your care,
that in stumbling we may not fall,
nor be overcome by evil,
but know that all shall be well, **Amen.**

Luke 13.31–35
Lent 2 (C); Mothering Sunday (ABC)

54. NOT LESS THAN EVERYTHING

God our lover,
in whose arms we are held,
and by whose passion we are known:
require of us also that love
which is filled with longing,
delights in the truth,
and costs not less than everything,
through Jesus Christ, **Amen.**

Isaiah 5.1–6; Hosea 11.1–9; Matthew 22.33–40; Mark 12.28–34;
Luke 10.25–28; 1 Corinthians 13
*Epiphany 4 (C); Proper 13 (C); Proper 22 (A); Proper 25 (A);
4 before Advent (B)*

55. OBEDIENCE AND RESISTANCE

Holy God,
by whose authority is judged
all human exercise of power,
give us grace to obey
where we are called to solidarity
and courage to resist
when your justice is at stake,
through Jesus Christ, **Amen.**

Amos 7.7–17; Mark 6.14–29
Proper 10 (BC)

56. ONE WITH THIS EARTH

God our creator,
you have made us one with this earth,
to tend it and to bring forth fruit:
may we so respect and cherish
all that has life from you,
that we may share in the labour of all creation
to give birth to your hidden glory,
through Jesus Christ, **Amen.**

Genesis 1.1–3, 24–31; 2.4–9; Romans 8.18–25
2 before Lent (AC); Harvest Thanksgiving

57. OUR NEIGHBOURS AS OURSELVES

Holy God,
whose name is not honoured
where the needy are not served,
and the powerless are treated with contempt:
may we embrace our neighbour
with the same tenderness
that we ourselves require;
so your justice may be fulfilled in love,
through Jesus Christ, **Amen.**

Leviticus 19.9–18; Amos 8.4–7; Luke 10.25–37; 16.19–end;
James 2.14–17; 1 John 4.7–21
*Proper 3 (A); Easter 5 (C); Proper 10 (BC); Proper 11 (C);
Proper 18 (B); Proper 19 (A); Proper 20 (C); Proper 21 (C);
4 before Advent (AC)*

58. OUR TENDER SHEPHERD

O Christ our tender Shepherd,
you know how anxious we are
and how easily we stray.
Let us hear your voice
above the clamour of all others,
that we may learn who truly feeds us
and find our way home to you,
our loving Lord, **Amen.**

Psalm 23; John 10.1–30
Easter 4 (ABC)

59. PARABLES

Christ our teacher,
you reach into our lives
not through instruction, but story.
Open our hearts to be attentive:
that seeing, we may perceive,
and hearing, we may understand,
and understanding, may act upon your word,
in your name, **Amen.**

Mark 4.1–20
Proper 10 (A); Proper 12 (AC)

60. POUR OUT YOUR SPIRIT

Spirit of energy and change,
in whose power Jesus was anointed
to be the hope of the nations:
be poured out also upon us
without reserve or distinction,
that we may have confidence and strength
to plant your justice on the earth,
through Jesus Christ, **Amen.**

Isaiah 42.1–7; Joel 2.28–29; Matthew 3.13–end
Baptism of Christ (ABC); Proper 25 (C)

61. POURED OUT LIKE PERFUME

Christ Jesus,
whose glory was poured out like perfume,
and who chose for our sake
to take the form of a slave:
may we also pour out our love
with holy extravagance,
that our lives may be fragrant with you, **Amen.**

Mark 14.3–9; Luke 7.36–end; John 12.1–8; Ephesians 4.25—5.2;
Philippians 2.1–11
Lent 5 (C); Palm Sunday; Proper 6 (C); Proper 14 (B);
Proper 21 (A); Holy Cross

62. SACRED SPACE

Holy God,
whose presence is known
in the structures we build,
and also in their collapse;
establish in us a community of hope,
not to contain your mystery,
but to be led beyond security
into your sacred space,
through Jesus Christ, **Amen.**

1 Kings 8.22–30; Jeremiah 7.1–11; Mark 13.1–8; Luke 21.5–19;
John 2.13–22; 1 Corinthians 3.10–17
Proper 3 (A); Lent 3 (B); Proper 4 (ABC); 2 before Advent (BC);
Dedication (ABC)

63. SEARCH US OUT

O God, lover of sinners,
you celebrate our return
as a woman rejoices with her friends.
Where we are lost, search us out,
and where we are locked away,
claim us for your own;
that together we may adorn
the beauty of your face,
through Jesus Christ, **Amen.**

Luke 15.1–10
Proper 19 (C)

64. SEARCHING THE DEPTHS

O God,
you have searched the depths we cannot know,
and touched what we cannot bear to name:
may we so wait,
enclosed in your darkness,
that we are ready to encounter
the terror of the dawn,
with Jesus Christ, **Amen.**

Job 14.1–14; Psalm 139
Epiphany 2 (B); Easter Vigil (ABC); Proper 4 (B); Proper 11 (A);
Proper 18 (C)

65. SHOCK OF THE SPIRIT

Spirit of truth
whom the world can never grasp,
touch our hearts
with the shock of your coming;
fill us with desire
for your disturbing peace;
and fire us with longing
to speak your uncontainable word
through Jesus Christ, **Amen.**

John 14.15–29; 20.19–23; Acts 2.1–21
Easter 2 (ABC); Easter 6 (AC); Pentecost (ABC)

66. SONGS OF LIBERATION

O God our deliverer,
you cast down the mighty,
and lift up those of no account:
as Elizabeth and Mary embraced
with songs of liberation,
so may we also be pregnant with your Spirit,
and affirm one another in hope for the world,
through Jesus Christ, **Amen.**

Luke 1.39–49
Advent 4 (C); Visitation (ABC)

67. STRENGTH MADE PERFECT IN WEAKNESS

O God against whom we struggle,
you speak with the voice of the persecuted
and call the oppressor to turn to you:
confront in us the violence
that we enact or consent to,
that our strength may be made perfect
in weakness,
and we may put our trust in you,
through Jesus Christ, **Amen.**

> Acts 9.1–22; 26.9–20; 2 Corinthians 12.7–10; Galatians 1.11–end
> *Easter 3 (C); Proper 5 (C); Proper 9 (B); Conversion of Paul (ABC)*

68. TELL OUT MY SOUL

O God whose word is fruitless
where the mighty are not put down,
the humble remain humiliated.
the hungry are not filled,
and the rich are:
make good your word,
and begin with us.
Open our hearts and unblock our ears
to hear the voices of the poor
and share their struggle;
and send us away empty with longing
for your promises to come true
in Jesus Christ. **Amen.**

> Luke 1.46–55
> *Blessed Virgin Mary (ABC); Advent 3 (AB); Advent 4 (BC);*
> *Proper 21 (C)*

69. THE BURDEN OF LOVE

O God,
you took upon you
the yoke of humanity
and the burden of love,
and did not find it easy:
let us learn from you
to share the weight
of all this aching world,
that our souls may be light,
and our hearts rested,
as together we are carried by you
in Jesus Christ, **Amen.**

Matthew 11.18–30
Proper 9 (A)

70. THE FOOLISH WISDOM OF GOD

Hidden God,
whose wisdom compels our love
and unsettles all our values;
fill us with desire
to search for her truth,
that we may transform the world
becoming fools for her sake,
through Jesus Christ, **Amen.**

Proverbs 1.20–33; 2.1–9; Matthew 11.25–30; Luke 10.30–42;
1 Corinthians 1.18–25; 3.18–end
*Epiphany 4 (A); Proper 3 (AC); 2 before Lent (B); Lent 3 (B);
Proper 9 (A); Proper 11 (C); Proper 19 (BC)*

71. THE FORGIVING FATHER

God our father,
you disarm our judgement
with your outrageous mercy;
and the punishment we seek
you turn to celebration.
Lift our self-loathing,
and embrace our stubbornness,
that we too may show such fathering
to an embittered world,
through Jesus Christ, **Amen.**

Luke 15.11–end
Lent 4 (C)

72. THE OUTSIDER

O God whose word is life,
and whose delight is to answer our cry,
give us faith like the Syro-Phoenician woman,
who refused to remain an outsider:
that we too may have the wit to argue
and demand that our daughters be made whole,
through Jesus Christ, **Amen.**

Matthew 15.2–28; Mark 7.24–end
Proper 5 (A); Proper 15 (A); Proper 18 (B)

73. THE REFINING FIRE

God our healer,
whose mercy is like a refining fire:
touch us with your judgement,
and confront us with your tenderness;
that, being comforted by you,
we may reach out to a troubled world,
through Jesus Christ, **Amen.**

Isaiah 40.1–11; Malachi 3.1–5
Advent 2 (ABC); Proper 2 (B); Proper 23 (BC); Proper 25 (B);
Presentation (ABC); Birth of John the Baptist (ABC)

74. THE STILL, SMALL VOICE

O God from whom we flee,
whose stillness is more terrible
than earthquake, wind, or fire,
speak to our loneliness
and challenge our despair:
that in your very absence
we may recognize your voice,
and wrapped in your presence
we may go forth to encounter the world,
in the name of Christ, **Amen.**

1 Kings 19.9–18
Proper 7 (C); Proper 14 (A)

75. THE VISION OF GOD

O God,
whose beauty is beyond our imagining,
and whose power we cannot comprehend:
show us your glory
as far as we can grasp it,
and shield us
from knowing more than we can bear
until we may look upon you without fear,
through Jesus Christ, **Amen.**

> Genesis 32.22–31; Exodus 33.12–end; Job 38.1–7, 34–41
> *Proper 13 (A); Proper 24 (ABC)*

76. THE WAY OF PEACE/APOCALYPSE

Spirit of truth and judgement,
who alone can exorcize
the powers that grip our world:
at the point of crisis
give us your discernment,
that we may accurately name what is evil,
and know the way that leads to peace,
through Jesus Christ, **Amen.**

> Matthew 12.22–32; Mark 3.22–27; Luke 13.33–34; 19.41–end;
> 21.5–19; Ephesians 6.10–20
> *Lent 2 (BC); Proper 5 (B); Proper 16 (B); Proper 22 (A);*
> *2 before Advent (C)*

77. TRANSFIGURATION

Christ, our only true light,
before whose bright cloud
your friends fell to the ground:
we bow before your cross
that we may refuse to be prostrated
before the false brightness of any other light,
looking to your power alone
for hope of resurrection from the dead, **Amen.**

Matthew 17.1–13; Mark 9.2–13; Luke 9.28–36
Sunday next before Lent (ABC); The Transfiguration of Our Lord

78. TRINITY OF LOVE

O God our mystery,
you bring us to life,
call us to freedom,
and move between us with love.
May we so participate
in the dance of your trinity,
that our lives may resonate with you,
now and for ever, **Amen.**

Genesis 1.1—2.4a
Trinity Sunday (ABC)

79. TURN FROM OUR GUILT

O God,
you have made us for yourself,
and against your longing there is no defence.
Mark us with your love,
and release in us a passion for your justice
in our disfigured world;
that we may turn from our guilt and face you,
our heart's desire, **Amen.**

Isaiah 58.1–8; Matthew 6.16–21
Proper 1 (A); Ash Wednesday (ABC); Proper 22 (AB)

80. WASHING FEET

Christ, whose feet were caressed
with perfume and a woman's hair;
you humbly took basin and towel
and washed the feet of your friends.
Wash us also in your tenderness
as we touch one another:
that, embracing your service freely,
we may accept no other bondage
in your name, **Amen.**

John 12.1–11; 13.1–15
*Lent 5 (C); Monday in Holy Week (ABC); Maundy Thursday (ABC);
2 before Advent (C)*

81. WE CONSTANTLY BETRAY

God, our hope of victory
whom we constantly betray;
grant us so to recognize your coming
that in our clamour
there may be commitment,
and in our silence
the very stones may cry aloud
in your name, **Amen.**

Matthew 21.1–13; Mark 14.32—15.41; Luke 19.28–40
Palm Sunday (ABC)

82. WHO IS THE GREATEST?

Christ our Lord,
you refused the way of domination
and died the death of a slave.
May we also refuse to lord it
over those who are subject to us,
but share the weight of authority
so that all may be empowered
in your name, **Amen.**

Mark 10.33–45
Proper 20 (B); Proper 24 (B)

83. WHOLE ARMOUR OF FAITH

God our security,
who alone can defend us
against the principalities and powers
that rule this present age:
may we trust in no weapons
except the whole armour of faith,
that in dying we may live,
and, having nothing,
we may own the world,
through Jesus Christ, **Amen.**

> Romans 13.8–14; 2 Corinthians 6.1–13; Ephesians 6.10–20
> *Proper 7 (AB); Proper 16 (B); Proper 18 (A)*

84. WORK AND FAITH

God of wholeness,
you have created us bodily,
that our work and faith may be one.
May we offer our worship
from lives of integrity;
and maintain the fabric of this world
with hearts that are set on you,
through Jesus Christ, **Amen.**

> Ecclesiasticus/Ben Sirach 38.24–end

85. WRESTLING WITH GOD

O God, with whom we wrestle
until the break of day,
make us long to seek your face
beyond the limits of our strength:
that in our wounds we may remember you,
and in your blessing
we may find our selves,
through Jesus Christ, **Amen.**

Genesis 32.22–31
Proper 13 (A); Proper 24 (C)

Scripture Index

References are to collect number

Common Worship Lectionary Index

Formal Prayers

Canticles, Confessions, Eucharistic Prayers

TE DEUM

We long for you O God,
we confess our deep desire;
for the heavens are arrayed
with your unhidden beauty,
and the entire earth
surrenders to your touch.

The powers of everlasting light
cry aloud to you;
the holy and ancient places of darkness
continually cry your name.

Saints in every generation
speak your outrageous glory;
those who have seen and proclaimed you
are passionate with praise;
those who have cried for justice
are satisfied in you;
those who carried you in their wounds
are bodied forth with life.
Your holy and stumbling church
throughout all the world
is filled with your desire.

Merciful creator, of an infinite tenderness;
wounded redeemer, by whom all flesh is moved;
comforter of fire, who leads us into truth;
God difficult and beautiful,
we offer you our praise.

You are the source of our yearning O Christ:
you are the way of glory.
Bearing our sweet and humble flesh,

fruit of a woman's womb,
you were made and moulded as we are
by human particular touch.

Breaking forth from the tomb
you opened wide our hearts,
turning the sharpness of death
to the terror of new life
and of desire fulfilled.

We believe that you will come,
our lover and our judge:
increase our longing for justice
in your afflicted world,
that we may be counted among your saints in glory,
and know ourselves beloved.

Spirit of discernment
integrity and fire:
breathe on our fearfulness,
refine our truthfulness,
and sing through our speechlessness;
that we may daily refuse what is evil,
and be taken up with praise.

O God, I have poured out my longing before you,
I have abandoned myself.
All that I am lies open to your touch;
let me never be put to shame.

GLORIA

Glory be to God on high,
and on earth peace,
peace among those of good will.
We praise you, we bless you,
we worship you, we glorify you,
we give you thanks for your great glory,
holy God, tender God, God our beloved creator.

Christ our desire,
only embodiment of God,
bone of our bone and flesh of our flesh,
foolishness of God, greater than human wisdom,
poverty of God, stronger than human pride,
emptiness of God, full of our redemption,
bearing away the sin of the world,
have mercy upon us.
Holy one, bearing away the sin of the world,
have mercy upon us.
Beloved one, bearing away the sin of the world,
receive our prayer.

For you alone are holy,
you alone our desire.
You alone, O Christ,
with the comforter of fire,
are radiant with the grace and glory of God most high.

HYMN TO WISDOM

My soul yearns for wisdom,
and beyond all else my heart longs for her.
She has walked through the depths of the abyss,
she has measured its boundaries;
for she was there from the beginning,
and apart from her, not one thing came to be.
She played before creation, when the world was made,
and in her hands are all things held together;
she has danced upon the face of the deep,
and all that has breath is instinct with her life.
The mystery of creation is in her grasp,
yet she delights to expound her ways.

In the streets of the city, wisdom is calling,
and on the access roads she encounters those who pass;
at the gates of the camp she sings in triumph,
and in the law courts she lifts up her voice.
With the timid and fearful she takes her stand,

and in the mouths of children she is heard to speak.
She cries out to the foolish to listen,
and the wise take heed to her words.
But among her own, she is not recognized,
and those who need her have thrust her out;
she has been pushed aside like the poor,
and broken like those of no account.

So she abandons those who are wise in their own sight,
but with all who are ready to receive her,
she makes her home.
For her delight is in the truth,
and she takes no pleasure in deceitful ways;
her integrity is more to be desired than comfort,
and her discernment is more precious than security.
In her alone is the life of humanity,
therefore while I live I will search her out;
for whoever is fed by wisdom will never hunger,
and all who drink from her will never thirst again.

This hymn was written as a reflection upon a meeting of the *Peace Preaching Course*, on the theme '*And the Word was made flesh*', held in Oxford, July 1987.

It may be read antiphonally, each voice taking two lines alternately.

BENEDICITE OMNIA OPERA

All you works of God, bless your creator;
praise her and glorify her for ever.

Let the wide earth bless the creator;
let the arching heavens bless the creator;
let the whole body of God bless the creator;
praise her and glorify her for ever.

You returning daylight, bless your creator;
twilight and shadows, bless your creator;
embracing darkness, bless your creator;
praise her and glorify her for ever.

Mountains of God, massive and ancient rocks,
bless your creator;
valleys and pastures, moorland and rivers,
bless your creator;
ocean depths and lonely abyss,
bless your creator;
praise her and glorify her for ever.

Storm and mighty wind, bless your creator;
bitter cold and scorching sun, bless your creator;
mist and cloud and tender rain,
bless your creator;
praise her and glorify her for ever.

Seed and sapling, tree and vivid flower,
bless your creator;
greenness and flourishing,
withering and bareness, bless your creator;
harvest and springtime and deadness of the year,
bless your creator;
praise her and glorify her for ever.

You creatures of God, bless your creator;
swift and cunning, violent and graceful,
bless your creator;
all who creep and soar and dance across the earth,
bless your creator;
praise her and glorify her for ever.

You newborn babies, bless your creator;
young and old, mature and ageing,
bless your creator;
all you dying, bless your creator;
praise her and glorify her for ever.

In pain and desolation, let us bless our creator;
in the place of delight, let us bless our creator;
in time of waiting, let us bless our creator;
praise her and glorify her for ever.

Let all who live and grow and breathe
bless our creator,
praise her and glorify her for ever.

This canticle was first used at the Greenham vigil, August 1987.

STATEMENT OF FAITH

O God, the source of our being
and the goal of all our longing,
we believe and trust in you.
The whole earth is alive with your glory,
and all that has life is sustained by you.
We commit ourselves to cherish your world,
and to seek your face.

O God, embodied in a human life,
we believe and trust in you.
Jesus our brother, born of the woman Mary,
you confronted the proud and the powerful,
and welcomed as your friends
those of no account.
Holy Wisdom of God, firstborn of creation,
you emptied yourself of power,
and became foolishness for our sake.
You laboured with us upon the cross,
and have brought us forth
to the hope of resurrection.
We commit ourselves to struggle against evil
and to choose life.

O God, life-giving Spirit,
Spirit of healing and comfort,
of integrity and truth,
we believe and trust in you.
Warm-winged Spirit, brooding over creation,
rushing wind and Pentecostal fire,
we commit ourselves to work with you
and renew our world.

> This statement of faith, and the confession that follows, were
> written and revised for regular use in the *Women in Theology*
> liturgy group.

CONFESSION AND MUTUAL ABSOLUTION

O God, you have searched us out and known us,
and all that we are is open to you.
We confess that we have sinned:
we have used our power to dominate
    and our weakness to manipulate;
we have evaded responsibility
    and failed to confront evil;
we have denied dignity
        to ourselves and to our sisters *(each other)*,
    and fallen into despair.

**We turn to you, O God;
we renounce evil;
we claim your love;
we choose to be made whole.**

*(In turn, around the circle, we say for each other:
'Woman/man, your sins are forgiven; be at peace.' This can be
accompanied by a gesture such as taking hands, or making the
sign of the cross on the forehead.)*

CONFESSION

O Christ,
in whose body was named
all the violence of the world,
and in whose memory is contained
our profoundest grief,

we lay open to you:
the violence done to us in time before memory;
the unremembered wounds that have misshaped our lives;
the injuries we cannot forget and have not forgiven.

The remembrance of them is grievous to us;
the burden of them is intolerable.

We lay open to you:
the violence done in our name in time before memory;
the unremembered wounds we have inflicted;
the injuries we cannot forget and for which we have not
been forgiven.

The remembrance of them is grievous to us;
the burden of them is intolerable.

We lay open to you:
those who have pursued a violent knowledge the world
cannot forget;
those caught up in violence they have refused to name;
those who have enacted violence which they have not
repented.

The remembrance of them is grievous to us;
the burden of them is intolerable.

We lay open to you:
the victims of violence whose only memorial is our anger;
those whose suffering was sustained on our behalf;
those whose continued oppression provides the ground we
stand on.

The remembrance of them is grievous to us;
the burden of them is intolerable.

Hear what comfortable words our saviour Christ says to all
who truly turn to God:

Come to me, all you who labour and are heavy-laden,
and I will give you rest.
Take my yoke upon you, and learn from me,
for I am gentle and lowly in heart,
and you will find rest for your souls.
For my yoke is easy, and my burden is light.

**We wholeheartedly repent
of the evil we have done,
and of the evil done on our behalf;
and we look for grace to offer forgiveness,
and to know ourselves forgiven.**

GOOD FRIDAY REPROACHES

Holy God,
holy and strange,
holy and intimate,
have mercy on us.

O my people, what have I done to you?
How have I offended you?
Answer me.

I brooded over the abyss,
with my words I called forth creation:
but you have brooded on destruction,
and manufactured the means of chaos.

O my people, what have I done to you?
How have I offended you?
Answer me.

I breathed life into your bodies,
and carried you tenderly in my arms:
but you have armed yourselves for war,
breathing out threats of violence.

O my people, what have I done to you?
How have I offended you?
Answer me.

I made the desert blossom before you,
I fed you with an open hand:
but you have grasped the children's food,
and laid waste fertile lands.

O my people, what have I done to you?
How have I offended you?
Answer me.

I abandoned my power like a garment,
choosing your unprotected flesh:

but you have robed yourselves in privilege,
and chosen to despise the abandoned.

O my people, what have I done to you?
How have I offended you?
Answer me.

Holy God,
holy and strange,
holy and intimate,
have mercy on us.

I would have gathered you to me as a lover,
and shown you the ways of peace:
but you have desired security,
and you would not surrender your self.

O my people, what have I done to you?
How have I offended you?
Answer me.

I have torn the veil of my glory,
transfiguring the earth:
but you have disfigured my beauty,
and turned away your face.

O my people, what have I done to you?
How have I offended you?
Answer me.

I have laboured to deliver you,
as a woman delights to give life:
but you have delighted in bloodshed,
and laboured to bereave the world.

O my people, what have I done to you?
How have I offended you?
Answer me.

I have followed you with the power of my spirit,
to seek truth and heal the oppressed:

but you have been following a lie,
and returned to your own comfort.

O my people, what have I done to you?
How have I offended you?
Answer me.

Holy God,
holy and strange,
holy and intimate,
have mercy on us.

Genesis 1; 2.7; Psalm 22.9–10; 104.28; Isaiah 35.1; 46.3–4; 53.1–4;
Matthew 27.51; Luke 13.34; 19.41–44; John 16.20–22

EUCHARISTIC PRAYER FOR ORDINARY USE

Eternal Wisdom, source of our being,
and goal of all our longing,
we praise you and give you thanks
because you have created us, women and men,
together in your image
to cherish your world and seek your face.
Divided and disfigured by sin,
while we were yet helpless,
you emptied yourself of power,
and took upon you our unprotected flesh.
You laboured with us upon the cross,
and have brought us forth
to the hope of resurrection.

Therefore, with the woman who gave you birth,
the women who befriended you and fed you,
who argued with you and touched you,
the woman who anointed you for death,
the women who met you, risen from the dead,
and with all your lovers throughout the ages,
we praise you saying:

Holy, holy, holy,
vulnerable God,
heaven and earth are full of your glory;
hosanna in the highest.
Blessed is the one
who comes in the name of God;
hosanna in the highest.

Blessed is our brother Jesus,
who, before his suffering, earnestly desired
to eat with his companions
the passover of liberation;
who, on the night that he was betrayed,
took bread, gave thanks, broke it, and said:
'This is my body, which is for you.
Do this to remember me.'
In the same way also the cup, after supper, saying:
'This cup is the new covenant in my blood.
Do this, whenever you drink it,
to remember me.'

Christ has died.
Christ is risen.
Christ will come again.

Therefore, as we eat this bread and drink this cup,
we are proclaiming Christ's death until he comes.
In the body broken and the blood poured out,
we restore to memory and hope
the broken and unremembered victims
of tyranny and sin;
and we long for the bread of tomorrow
and the wine of the age to come.
Come then, life-giving spirit of our God,
brood over these bodily things,
and make us one body with Christ;
that we may labour with creation
to be delivered from its bondage to decay
into the glorious liberty
of all the children of God.

EUCHARISTIC PRAYER FOR CHRISTMAS EVE

O Eternal Wisdom,
we praise you and give you thanks,
because you emptied yourself of power
and became foolishness for our sake:
for on this night you were delivered as one of us,
a baby needy and naked,
wrapped in a woman's blood;
born into poverty and exile,
to proclaim the good news to the poor,
and to let the broken victims go free.

Therefore, with the woman who gave you birth,
the women who befriended you and fed you,
who argued with you and touched you,
the woman who anointed you for death,
the women who met you, risen from the dead,
and with all your lovers throughout the ages,
we praise you, saying:

**Holy, holy, holy,
vulnerable God,
heaven and earth are full of your glory;
hosanna in the highest.
Blessed is the one
who comes in the name of God;
hosanna in the highest.**

Blessed is our brother Jesus,
bone of our bone and flesh of our flesh;
who, on the night when he was delivered over to death,
took bread, gave thanks, broke it, and said:
'This is my body, which is for you.
Do this to remember me.'
In the same way also the cup, after supper, saying:
'This cup is the new covenant in my blood.
Do this, whenever you drink it,
to remember me.'
For, as we eat this bread and drink this cup,
we are proclaiming the Lord's death until he comes.

Christ has died.
Christ is risen.
Christ will come again.

Come now, dearest Spirit of God,
embrace us with your comfortable power.
Brood over these bodily things,
and make us one body in Christ.
As Mary's body was broken for him,
and her blood shed,
so may we show forth his brokenness
for the life of the world,
and may creation be made whole
through the new birth in his blood.

> This prayer was written for a eucharistic celebration on Christmas
> Eve 1986, at Holy Trinity House, Paddington, attended only by
> women. A woman priest presided. The poem *That night we gathered*
> (p. 108) was written after this occasion.

FOOTWASHING LITURGY FOR MAUNDY THURSDAY

O Eternal Wisdom,
we praise you and give you thanks,
because you laid aside your power as a garment,
and took upon you the form of a slave.
You became obedient unto death,
even death on a cross,
receiving authority and comfort
from the hands of a woman;
for God chose what is weak in the world
to shame the strong,
and God chose what is low and despised in the world,
even things that are not,
to bring to nothing things that are.

Therefore, with the woman who gave you birth,
the women who befriended you and fed you,
who argued with you and touched you,
the woman who anointed you for death,
the women who met you, risen from the dead,
and with all your lovers throughout the ages,
we praise you saying:

**Holy, holy, holy,
vulnerable God,
heaven and earth are full of your glory;
hosanna in the highest.
Blessed is the one
who comes in the name of God;
hosanna in the highest.**

Blessed is our brother Jesus,
who on this night, before Passover,
rose from supper, laid aside his garments,
took a towel and poured water,
and washed his disciples' feet, saying to them:
'If I, your Lord and Teacher,
have washed your feet,
you also ought to wash one another's feet.
If you know these things,
blessed are you if you do them.
If I do not wash you,
you have no part in me.'

**Lord, not my feet only
but also my hands and my head.**

Come now, tender spirit of our God,
wash us and make us one body in Christ;
that, as we are bound together
in this gesture of love,
we may no longer be in bondage
to the principalities and powers
that enslave creation,

but may know your liberating peace
such as the world cannot give.

(This prayer is followed by the mutual washing of feet.)

> This liturgy was first used at the Greenham vigil, on Maundy
> Thursday 1987, by a group of Christian women at Blue Gate,
> Greenham Common. It was followed by a Passover meal.

EUCHARISTIC PRAYER FOR GOOD FRIDAY

O holy Wisdom of our God,
eternally offensive to our wisdom,
and compassionate towards our weakness,
we praise you and give you thanks,
because you emptied yourself of power
and entered our struggle,
taking upon you our unprotected flesh.
You opened wide your arms for us upon the cross,
becoming scandal for our sake,
that you might sanctify even the grave
to be a bed of hope to your people.

Therefore, with those who are detained without justice,
abandoned or betrayed by friends,
whose bodies are violated or in pain;
with those who have died alone
without dignity, comfort, or hope;
and with all the company of saints
who have carried you in their wounds
that they may be bodied forth with life,
we praise you, saying:

**Holy, holy, holy,
vulnerable God.
Heaven and earth are full of your glory;
hosanna in the highest.
Blessed is the one**

who comes in the name of God;
hosanna in the highest.

Blessed is our brother Jesus,
bone of our bone and flesh of our flesh,
from whom the cup of suffering did not pass;
who, on the night that he was betrayed,
took bread, gave thanks, broke it, and said:
'This is my body, which is for you.
Do this to remember me.'
In the same way also the cup, after supper, saying:
'This cup is the new covenant in my blood.
Do this, whenever you drink it,
to remember me.'

Christ has died.
Christ is risen.
Christ will come again.

Therefore, as we eat this bread and drink this cup,
we are proclaiming Christ's death until he comes.
In the body broken and the blood poured out,
we restore to memory and hope
the broken and unremembered victims
of tyranny and sin;
and we long for the bread of tomorrow,
and the wine of the age to come.
Come then, life-giving spirit of our God,
brood over these bodily things,
and make us one body with Christ,
that we, who are baptized into his death
may walk in newness of life;
that what is sown in dishonour
may be raised in glory,
and what is sown in weakness
may be raised in power.

Genesis 2.23; Matthew 6.11; 1 Corinthians 1.23; 15.42–43;
2 Corinthians 5.21; Philippians 2.1–11

This prayer was first used on Good Friday 1989 at Salisbury and
Wells Theological College.

EUCHARISTIC PRAYER FOR EASTER

O Eternal Wisdom,
we praise you and give you thanks,
because the beauty of death
could not contain you.
You broke forth from the comfort of the grave;
before you the stone was moved,
and the tomb of our world was opened wide.
For on this day you were raised in power
and revealed yourself to women
as a beloved stranger,
offering for the rituals of the dead
the terror of new life
and of desire fulfilled.

Therefore, with the woman who gave you birth,
the women who befriended you and fed you,
who argued with you and touched you,
the woman who anointed you for death,
the women who met you, risen from the dead,
and with all your lovers throughout the ages,
we praise you, saying:

**Holy, holy, holy,
resurrection God,
heaven and earth are full of your glory;
hosanna in the highest.
Blessed is the one
who comes in the name of God;
hosanna in the highest.**

Blessed is our brother Jesus,
who walks with us the road of our grief,
and is known again in the breaking of bread;
who, on the night he was handed over,
took bread, gave thanks, broke it, and said:
'This is my body, which is for you.
Do this to remember me.'
In the same way also the cup, after supper, saying:

'This cup is the new covenant in my blood.
Do this whenever you drink it,
to remember me.'

**Christ has died.
Christ is risen.
Christ will come again.**

Come now, disturbing spirit of our God,
breathe on these bodily things
and make us one body in Christ.
Open our graves, unbind our eyes,
and name us here;
touch and heal all that has been buried in us,
that we need not cling to our pain,
but may go forth with power
to release resurrection in the world.

This prayer was written for the St Hilda Community.
It was first used on Easter Day, 1987.

EUCHARISTIC PRAYER FOR PENTECOST

O Eternal Wisdom,
we praise you and give you thanks,
for, as you revealed yourself of old
in fire and storm and precious law,
so you did not leave your followers comfortless,
but came upon them on this day
in thunder, wind and flame,
filling them with clarity and power,
and making them drunk with longing
to utter your uncontainable word.
And now, you have poured out your spirit
upon all flesh,
that your sons and daughters may prophesy,
that old and young may share a vision,
and even the slaves find a voice.

Therefore,
with Elizabeth who prophesied your birth,
Mary who sang for the poor,
Martha who confessed you as the Christ,
the women who announced you
risen from the dead,
and with every nameless and unremembered prophet
who heard your call and inspired her people,
we praise you, saying:

**Holy, holy, holy,
God of power and might,
heaven and earth are full of your glory;
hosanna in the highest.
Blessed is the one
who comes in the name of God;
hosanna in the highest.**

Blessed is our brother Jesus,
who comes behind the doors we have closed,
and breathes on our fear his fearful peace;
who, on the night that he was betrayed,

took bread, gave thanks, broke it, and said:
'This is my body, which is for you.
Do this to remember me.'
In the same way the cup, after supper, saying:
'This cup is the new covenant in my blood.
Do this whenever you drink it,
to remember me.'

**We remember Christ's death;
we proclaim Christ's resurrection;
we await Christ's coming in glory.**

Come now, spirit of integrity,
of tenderness, judgement, and dance;
touch our speechlessness,
kindle our longing,
reach into our silence,
and fire our words with your truth;
that each may hear in her own language
the mighty works of God.

This prayer was written for the St Hilda Community. It was first
used at Pentecost, 1987.

Litanies

FOR THE DARKNESS OF WAITING

For the darkness of waiting
of not knowing what is to come
of staying ready and quiet and attentive,
we praise you O God:

**for the darkness and the light
are both alike to you.**

For the darkness of staying silent
for the terror of having nothing to say
and for the greater terror
of needing to say nothing,
we praise you O God:

**for the darkness and the light
are both alike to you.**

For the darkness of loving
in which it is safe to surrender
to let go of our self-protection
and to stop holding back our desire,
we praise you O God:

**for the darkness and the light
are both alike to you.**

For the darkness of choosing
when you give us the moment
to speak, and act, and change,
and we cannot know what we have set in motion,
but we still have to take the risk,
we praise you O God:

**for the darkness and the light
are both alike to you.**

For the darkness of hoping
in a world which longs for you,
for the wrestling and the labouring of all creation
for wholeness and justice and freedom,
we praise you O God:

**for the darkness and the light
are both alike to you.**

First written for the *Women in Theology* liturgy group, Advent
Sunday, 1985, this litany was also used in the *Liturgy of Hope*,
Canterbury Cathedral, 18 April 1986.

LITANY OF PENITENCE FOR THE DENIAL OF WOMEN'S AUTHORITY

Man: Let us confess our sins:
We have denied the authority of women
and limited their gifts;
we have locked away women's power,
and chosen to hide their pain.
But nothing is veiled that will not be revealed:

Men: **and nothing is hidden
that will not be made known.**

Woman: We have undermined the authority of women
and limited our gifts;
we have locked away women's power,
and chosen to hide our pain.
But nothing is veiled that will not be revealed:

Women: **and nothing is hidden
that will not be made known.**

Man: We have feared those who are not like us;
we have refused to know our weakness.
We have locked away part of ourselves.
But nothing is veiled that will not be revealed:

Men: and nothing is hidden
   that will not be made known.

Woman: We have feared those who are like us;
   we have refused to know our strength.
   We have locked away part of ourselves.
   But nothing is veiled that will not be revealed:

Women: and nothing is hidden
   that will not be made known.

Man: We have resisted the Wisdom of God
   and refused to seek her face.

Woman: We have turned aside from her image
   and hidden our knowledge of her.
   But have no fear:
   for nothing is veiled that will not be revealed:

All: and nothing is hidden
   that will not be made known.

This litany and the one that follows were written for a festival
service to mark the opening of holy orders to women in the Diocese
of London, on 31 March 1987, at the church of St Mary-le-Bow.

LITANY OF BLESSING FOR WOMEN
TAKING AUTHORITY

Woman: Blessed is she who believed there would be a
   fulfilment of what was spoken to her by the Lord.

Women: Blessed are you among women.

Man: May you speak with the voice of the voiceless, and
   give courage to those in despair.

Men: Blessed are you among women.

Woman: May you feed the hungry of mind and heart, and
send away satisfied those who are empty.

Women: **Blessed are you among women.**

Man: May you be strong to confront injustice, and
powerful to rebuke the arrogant.

Men: **Blessed are you among women.**

Woman: May you not be alone, but find support in your
struggle, and sisters to rejoice with you.

Women: **Blessed are you among women.**

Man: May your vision be fulfilled, in company with us;
may you have brothers on your journey.

Men: **Blessed are you among women.**

Woman: Blessed is she who believed there would be a
fulfilment of what was spoken to her by the Lord.

All: **Blessed are you among women.**

CHRIST OUR BELOVED
(Ruth and Naomi)

Christ our beloved,
whose persistent care for us
is painstaking and joyful;
to whom we are free to cling
without fear of refusal
or loss of who we are:

we celebrate those
who are willing to share the intimacy of their pain;
whose tough compassion surpasses common sense;
who choose commitment in the place of despair.

Surely goodness and steadfast love shall follow me
all the days of my life:
and I will dwell in the house of the Lord for ever.

We celebrate those times
when our hearts have sung with surrender;
when it has been easy and obvious to give ourselves;
when our love has been accepted.

Surely goodness and steadfast love shall follow me
all the days of my life;
and I will dwell in the house of the Lord for ever.

We celebrate those
who have been our companions on an unknown road;
who have declined to abandon us when bitterly invited;
whose arms have been for us the arms of God.

Surely goodness and steadfast love shall follow me
all the days of my life;
and I will dwell in the house of the Lord for ever.

Ruth 1

GOD OF POWER AND JOY
(Visitation)

God of power and joy,
of calling and vision and hope,
you have endowed us with limitless desire,
and sisters with whom to sing.

Let us bless our sisters:
whose greeting fills us with joy;
whose presence gives us speech;
whose love we acclaim with pride;
with whom we need hold back nothing.

Blessed is she who has believed
God's promise will be fulfilled.

Let us bless our sisters:
whose yearning leaps to greet our own;
who are not diminished by our power;
whose wisdom discerns our soul;
who embrace what we shall become.

Blessed is she who has believed
God's promise will be fulfilled.

Let us bless our sisters:
who have stirred us to new vision;
whose courage lets us act;
with whom we proclaim on the housetops
the dreams we have held in secret.

Blessed is she who has believed
God's promise will be fulfilled.

Luke 1.39–56

HOLY AND INCARNATE ONE
(Incarnation)

Holy and incarnate one,
at whose unexpected touch
the ordinary world
is charged with God:

we pray for those
whose hardship is overwhelming, who cannot find you;
who live in poverty, anxiety, and hunger;
whose lives are fearful or lonely;
who are exploited, exhausted or ill.

For the Word was made flesh
and dwelt among us.

We pray for those
whose ambition is overwhelming, who do not want to
find you;
whose lives are choked with overwork or consumption;
who have chosen an unreal path;
who have hardened their hearts.

For the Word was made flesh
and dwelt among us.

We pray for those
who have begun to find you, and are overwhelmed;
for whom the risk of healing is too painful;
who are afraid of your embrace,
and fear your energetic power
to reconstitute the world.

For the Word was made flesh
and dwelt among us.

John 1.14

GOD, INTIMATE AND FEARFUL
(Woman with haemorrhage)

O God, intimate and fearful,
who carried us with tenderness
within our mother's womb;
who appointed us to speak
when we were yet unborn:
touch our mouths with your truth,
and take away our fear,
that we may proclaim you to the nations
and celebrate your mighty acts:

Let the whole world see and know
that things which were cast down have been raised up
and things which had grown old have been made new.

Let us bless God for the women
whose blood has flowed that others might have life;
who have suffered at the hands of their allies;
who have refused to accept shame;
who have demanded healing.

Let the whole world see and know
that things which were cast down have been raised up
and things which had grown old have been made new.

Let us bless God for the women
who have boldly touched our lives;
who have disrupted our use of power;
who have made us see what was hidden,
and feel in our bodies what it means to be made whole.

Let the whole world see and know
that things which were cast down have been raised up
and things which had grown old have been made new.

Let us bless God for the women
who know what has been done to them;
whose courage leaves them exposed;
who, in fear and trembling and steadfast faith,
proclaim the whole truth of salvation.

Let the whole world see and know
that things which were cast down have been raised up
and things which had grown old have been made new.

Jeremiah 1.1–10; Mark 5.25–34

This litany was first used at a service held at St James's Piccadilly to celebrate the consecration of Barbara Harris in February 1989 – the first woman bishop in the Anglican Communion.

The versicle and response are taken from one of the collects used at the consecration itself.

O GOD OUR DELIVERER
(Woman bent double)

O God our deliverer,
at whose feet we are free
to lay down our heavy burden:

we bring before you
those whose tasks are back-breaking,
whose daily labour damages their bodies,
whose survival depends on repeating work that wounds
    them,
who cannot dance free.

Make them hear of joy and gladness;
that the bones which you have broken may rejoice.

We bring before you
those who live uneasy in their bodies,
those whose bodies restrict or pain them,
who are patronized by those who move with ease,
who cannot dance free.

Make them hear of joy and gladness;
that the bones which you have broken may rejoice.

We bring before you
those whose spirits are crushed,
who have forgotten how to look up with pride,
who have been long in bondage to oppression,
who cannot dance free.

Make them hear of joy and gladness;
that the bones which you have broken may rejoice.

Luke 13.10–17

GOD OUR BELOVED
(Simon the Pharisee and the woman who loved much)

God our beloved,
who alone can receive
the enormity of our love:
you embrace our yearning
and are not overwhelmed by our need.
Let us love you with all that we are,
and stretch us wider still.

When we are niggardly with our affection;
when we find refuge from fear in constraint,
and wantonly withhold our touch
from those who seek our welcome,
bless us with your shamelessness:

for though I give my body to be burned,
and have not charity,
it profits me nothing.

When what we know conceals from us our ignorance;
when we fail to discern you in those we disapprove of;
when our minds are blunted with lack of compassion,
so that we cannot see,
bless us with your tears:

for though I understand all mysteries and all
    knowledge,
and have not charity,
it profits me nothing.

When our generosity becomes ferocious;
when we demand that others receive what swamps them;
when we insist on being the only giver,
so that we cannot hear we are forgiven,
bless us with your surrender:

for though I give away all that I have,
and have not charity,
it profits me nothing.

Luke 7.36–50

GOD OF JUSTICE
(Persistent widow)

O God of justice,
you have called your prophets throughout the ages
to persist in proclamation
in the face of callousness,
and to be resilient in faith
confronting stupidity:

we pray for those
who have refused to be silent before injustice;
who have been repeatedly turned away but are not
    discouraged;
whose outrageous faith has caused the mighty to tremble;
whose stubborn humour gives their sisters* heart.

For the earth shall be full of the knowledge of God
as the waters cover the sea.

We pray for those
whose efforts in the cause of justice have left them damaged
    or bitter;
who are repudiated by those they struggled for;
who have lost all hope of remedy,
and whose voice is not heard.

For the earth shall be full of the knowledge of God
as the waters cover the sea.

We pray for those
who have the power to do good and will not;
who attend to no voice but their own;
who dismiss the causes of oppression,
and ignore the plight of the powerless.

For the earth shall be full of the knowledge of God
as the waters cover the sea.

*or 'allies' or 'brothers' as appropriate

Luke 18.1–8

O GOD OUR DESIRE
(Mary Magdalene)

O God our desire,
in the strangeness of searching
at a place beyond hope,
waiting to understand
what we cannot bear to think of,
we put our trust in you:

For death shall have no dominion.

In the strangeness of recognition
of the selves we have become
at the return of the beloved
when the face of love has changed,
we put our trust in you:

For death shall have no dominion.

In the strangeness of separation,
when we refrain from touching;
when we are blessed with freedom,
and invited to let go,
we put our trust in you:

For death shall have no dominion.

In the strangeness of joy,
when we are offered a new name,
a redeemed authority,
and a fresh surrender,
we put our trust in you:

For death shall have no dominion.

John 20.1–18

Short Prayers

MAY THE POWER OF GOD

May the power of God this day enable me,
the nakedness of God disarm me,
the beauty of God silence me,
the justice of God give me voice,
the integrity of God hold me,
the desire of God move me,
the fear of God expose me to the truth,
the breath of God give me abundant life.

CHRIST IN MY MIND

Christ in my mind
that I may see what is true;
Christ in my mouth
that I may speak with power;
Christ in my heart
that I may learn to be touched;
Christ in my hands
that I may work with tenderness;
Christ in my soul
that I may know my desire;
Christ in my arms
that I may embrace without fear;
Christ in my face
that I may shine with God.

BLESSED BE GOD

Blessed be God
who has not made me a man,
but created me a woman according to her will:
who sustains me with sisters;
who grounds me with friends;
who blesses me with desire;
and gives me to delight in women,
and to struggle with them,
for the enlarging of my soul
and the recovery of her world
to the glory of her holy name, **Amen.**

O THOU SUDDEN GOD

O thou sudden God,
generous in mercy
quickener of new life
giver of new love
irreverent, subversive,
deep source of yearning
startling comforter
bearer of darkness
unmaker of old paths
bringer of strange joy
abundant, disturbing,
healing unlooked for
tender and piercing:
late have I loved thee
O beauty so ancient and so new.

SING OUT MY SOUL

Sing out my soul,
sing of the holiness of God:
who has delighted in a woman,
lifted up the poor,
satisfied the hungry,
given voice to the silent,
grounded the oppressor,
blessed the full-bellied with emptiness,
and with the gift of tears
those who have never wept;
who has desired the darkness of the womb,
and inhabited our flesh.
Sing of the longing of God,
sing out, my soul.

Luke 1.39–53

TENDER GOD

Tender God,
you have seen my affliction,
and unbound my eyes;
you have bereaved me of the burden
to which I used to cling;
you have woven my pain
into patterns of integrity;
the wounds I cherished
you have turned into honours,
and the scars I kept hidden
into marks of truth.
You have touched me gently;
I have seen your face, and live.

YOU TOOK MY EXTRAVAGANCE

You took my extravagance,
and asked for passion;
you took my self-absorption,
and created insight;
you saw my need to give,
and called forth charity;
you accepted charity,
and made me long for justice.

GOD OF MY INTEGRITY

God of my integrity,
in whom knowledge of truth
and passion for justice are one;
my heart was sentimental and you cleansed it
with your rigorous mercy;
my thoughts were rigid and you engaged them
with your compassionate mind.
Heal my fragmented soul;
teach my naivety;
confront my laziness;
and inflame my longing
to know your loving discernment
and live out your active love,
through Jesus Christ, **Amen.**

MY HEART WAS WILDERNESS

My heart was wilderness
I heard your voice;
my grief divided me
you held me close;
bitterness consumed me
you overflowed with trust;
I longed to be with you
you let me stay.

YOU ARE HOME TO THE EXILE

You are home to the exile
touch to the frozen
daylight to the prisoner
authority to the silent
anger to the helpless
laughter to the weary
direction to the joyful:
come, our God, come.

FROM FEAR OF STAYING STILL

From fear of staying still, **O God deliver me.**
From fear of surrender, **O God deliver me.**
From fear of decision, **O God deliver me.**
From fear of losing respect, **O God deliver me.**
From fear of facing my fear, **O God deliver me.**
But from the fear that marks your presence,
I beseech you O God, do not deliver me.

GOD OF THE WEARY

God of the weary
receive my tiredness
God of the hungry
know my emptiness
God of those in danger
hold my fear
God of the silenced
hear my despair
God of the heavyladen
give me rest
God of the hopeful
fill me again with longing.

O GOD MY DARK MY SILENCE

O God my dark my silence
whose love enfolded me
before I breathed alone
whose hands caressed me
while I was still unformed
to whom I have been given
before my heart remembers
who knew me speechless
whose touch unmakes me
whose stillness finds me
for ever unprepared

SPIRIT OF COMFORT AND LONGING

Spirit of comfort and longing,
enfold my fear,
unclothe me of my pride,
unweave my thoughts,
uncomplicate my heart,
and give me surrender:
that I may tell my wounds,
lay down my work,
and greet the dark.

PRAYERS AT TIMES OF ENDING

O God our comfort and challenge,
whose presence is ever reliable
and ever unexpected:
grant us to grieve over what is ending
without falling into despair,
and to enter on our new vocation
without forgetting your voice,
through Jesus Christ, **Amen.**

Blessing for one laying down office

May the God who rested on the seventh day
to delight in all her creation,
hold you in her arms
as you have held this work,
celebrate with us
the life that takes life from you,
and give you grace to let go
into a new freedom, **Amen.**

For the dying

O God who brought us to birth,
and in whose arms we die:
we entrust to your embrace
our beloved *sister.*
Give *her* release from *her* pain,
courage to meet the darkness,
and grace to let go into new life,
through Jesus Christ, **Amen.**

At a funeral

O God who brought us to birth,
and in whose arms we die:
in our grief and shock
contain and comfort us;
embrace us with your love,
give us hope in our confusion,
and grace to let go into new life,
through Jesus Christ, **Amen.**

BLESSINGS

O God our dance,
in whom we live and move and have our being:
so direct our strength
and inspire our weakness
that we may enter with power
into the movement of your whole creation,
through our partner Jesus Christ, **Amen.**

May holy Wisdom,
kind to humanity,
steadfast, sure and free,
the breath of the power of God:
may she who makes all things new, in every age,
enter our souls,
and make us friends of God,
through Jesus Christ, **Amen.**

Easter

May the God who shakes heaven and earth,
whom death could not contain,
who lives to disturb and heal us,
bless you with power to go forth
and proclaim the gospel, **Amen.**

Pentecost

May the God who dances in creation,
who embraces us with human love,
who shakes our lives like thunder,
bless us and drive us out with power
to fill the world with her justice, **Amen.**

Psalms and Poems

Psalms

I WILL PRAISE GOD, MY BELOVED

I will praise God, my Beloved,
for she is altogether lovely.

Her presence satisfies my soul;
she fills my senses to overflowing
so that I cannot speak.

Her touch brings me to life;
the warmth of her hands makes me wholly alive.

Her embrace nourishes me, body and spirit;
every part of my being responds to her touch.

The beauty of her face is more than I can bear;
in her gaze I drown.

When she looks upon me
I can withhold nothing;

when she asks for my love
all my defences crumble;
my pride and my control are utterly dissolved.

O God I fear your terrible mercy;
I am afraid to surrender my self.

If I let go into the whirlpool of your love,
shall I survive the embrace?

If I fall into the strong currents of your desire,
shall I escape drowning?

But how shall I refuse my Beloved,
and how can I withdraw from the one my heart yearns for?

On the edge of your abyss I look down and I tremble;
but I will not stand gazing for ever.

Even in chaos you will bear me up;
if the waters go over my head,
you will still be holding me.

For the chaos is yours also,
and in the swirling of mighty waters
is your presence known.

If I trust her, surely her power will not fail me;
nor will she let me be utterly destroyed.

Though I lose all knowledge and all security,
yet will my God never forsake me;

but she will recreate me, in her steadfast love,
so that I need not be afraid.

Then will I praise my Beloved among the people,
among those who seek to know God.

GOD MY GOD, WHY HAVE YOU DESERTED ME?

God my God, why have you deserted me?
Why do I lie awake pleading,
when there is no one to hear me?

For my longing is more than I can bear,
my loneliness is like a yawning pit,
and my hunger is not filled.

For I said, I will seek my God and know her,
and she will answer me, and I shall be satisfied.

Behold, your word was before me and I sought you,
you opened my heart, so that I could not refuse your touch.
You reached your hand into the depths and drew me;
and my body flowed out with love.
I was given to you, body and soul;
I tendered my spirit and I held nothing back.

But you have seduced me O God, and I was seduced.
When I reached out to touch you,
my hands grasped emptiness;
I stretched out my arms and my heart,
and there was nothing to hold.

Why have I trusted in your word, O God?
Your word has become an agony to me,
and I cannot put it aside;
my mind searches it continually, but I find no rest.

But how can I say, I will forget her compassion;
and how can I return to my self,
as if her love had never been?
For the floods have passed through me,
and I have been changed;
the channels and gulleys remember the waters,
and they mourn;
the narrow places of my soul do not cease to hope for rain.

So I will remember my God, though she is far from me;
and though there is no one to hold me,
yet will I hold my heart open.

GOD IS MY STRONG ROCK IN WHOM I TRUST

God is my strong rock in whom I trust,
and all my confidence I rest in her.

Deep in my mother's womb, she knew me;
before my limbs were formed, she yearned for me.

Each of my movements she remembers with compassion,
and when I was still unseen, she did imagine me.

Her strength brought me forth into the light;
it was she who delivered me.
Hers were the hands that held me safe;
she cherished me upon my mother's breast.

When I stammer, she forms the words in my mouth,
and when I am silent, she has understood my thoughts.
If I shout and rage, she hears my plea and my uncertainty.

When I am afraid, she stays close to me,
and when I am full of terror, she does not hide her face.
If I struggle against her, she will contain me,
and when I resist her, she will match my strength.

But if I am complacent, she confronts me;
when I cling to falsehood, she undermines my pride;
for she is jealous for my integrity,
and her longing is for nothing less than truth.

To all who are weak she shows compassion,
and those who are downtrodden she causes to rise.
But she will confound the arrogant
at the height of their power,
and the oppressor she will throw to the ground;
the strategies of the hard-hearted she will utterly confute.

God pities the fallen, and I will love her;
she challenges the mighty,
and I desire her with my whole heart.
God is the rock in whom I put my trust,
and all my meaning is contained in her;
for without God there is no security,
and apart from her there is no place of safety.

AS A WOMAN IN LABOUR

As a woman in labour who longs for the birth,
I long for you, O God;
and as she is weary to see the face of her child,
so do I seek your deliverance.
She cries out, she pants, because her pain is great,
and her longing is beyond measure;
her whole body is groaning in travail
until she shall be delivered.

My soul hungers for you
as the child for her mother's breast;
like the infant who cries out in the night,
who waits in the dark to be comforted.
At night I will cry for your justice,
and in the morning I will seek you early;
for you O God are the source of my salvation,
and all my nourishment is found in you.

As a woman looks to her friend,
that she may open her heart and be free,
that her words may find understanding,
and her fears may be contained;
so do I look to you O God,
that you may search me and know my ways,
bringing me judgement and tenderness,
and sending me home released.

As the body of the lover yearns for her beloved,
so is my desire for your touch.
She cries out from her depths, she weeps,
and cannot speak
because of the beauty of her beloved.
You also have laid your hand upon me,
and I cannot forget your ways.

So I will cry for my Beloved, and I will not rest,
until I dwell in the darkness of her embrace,
and all my silence is enclosed in her.

O MY GOD, TURN TO ME
(Woman with haemorrhage)

O my God, turn to me;
answer my pain and my pleading,
for I am heavy with fear.
My fear has been my garment day and night;
anxiety clings to me like a shadow,
faithful and pitiless.

My blood flows like tears,
like weeping that will not end;
like grief that cannot be healed,
my body is drained of strength,
and I cannot contain myself.

Many draw back from me;
my friends withhold their touch.
Like a body that is untouched,
I have no substance;
like a dead thing that may not be touched,
I have become unclean.

But you have seen my reproach;
you comprehend my shame.
You alone are my helper,
in the shadow of your cloak I shall be healed.
I will not let you pass,
but I shall be comforted;
my soul clings to you,
and my affliction shall cease.

For I will touch you, and you shall know me;
you shall be moved by me.
In the flood of your power I shall be changed,
for you cannot withhold your love.
Every part of my being
reaches out for your touch;
and I shall know in my body
that I have been made whole.

Then shall my terror and trembling
be turned to the fear of God;
then shall my blood be the blood of life,
and my tears not grief, but grace.

Mark 5.25–34

I WAITED PATIENTLY FOR YOU
(Martha and Lazarus)

I waited patiently for you, O God,
but you did not hear me;
I prayed earnestly, and you took no heed.
In time of trouble, you were very absent,
and in my desolation, you abandoned me.

In my anger I cried out against you;
I could not forgive you.
For you abandoned your beloved friend,
you gave my brother over to the grip of death.
His pain consumed him, body and soul,
and you were not there;
his blood cried out from the ground,
and you were still unmoved.

Who are you, O God, that you should not weep?
And what is your power, that you stand idly by?
Where is your compassion, that it flows not for the needy,
and your heart, that it is not broken by the pleading of the
    poor?

Yet in the midst of my despair you challenged me,
and when I had no hope, you required me to speak.
My heart was ashes, and you promised life;
my mouth was full of bitterness,
and you drew forth words of faith.

For you address the powers of death;
like a woman in labour, you cry out.
At the sound of your voice
even the dead are shaken;
those forgotten by God
are compelled to another birth.
My brother came forth from the pit;
he could not refuse your voice.
Blind in his graveclothes and terror,
he did not withhold his love,
but he has come back to be unbound;
he has received resurrection.

So I will praise my God
who reaches into the grave;
and those who wait on the edge of the dark
shall open their hearts and sing.

John 11.1–44

IN THE MIDST OF THE COMPANY
(Jesus and the woman who anointed his head)

In the midst of the company I sat alone,
and the hand of death took hold of me;
I was cold with secrecy,
and my God was far away.

For this fear did my mother conceive me,
and to seek this pain did I come forth?
Did her womb nourish me for the dust,
or her breasts, for me to drink bitterness?

O that my beloved would hold me
and gather me in her arms;
that the darkness of God might comfort me,
that this cup might pass me by.

I was desolate, and she came to me;
when there was neither hope nor help for pain
she was at my side;
in the shadow of the grave she has restored me.

My cup was spilling with betrayal,
but she has filled it with wine;
my face was wet with fear,
but she has anointed me with oil,
and my hair is damp with myrrh.
The scent of her love surrounds me;
it is more than I can bear.

She has touched me with authority;
in her hands I find strength.
For she acts on behalf of the broken,
and her silence is the voice of the unheard.
Though many murmur against her, I will praise her;
and in the name of the unremembered,
I will remember her.

Mark 14.1–9

O GOD HEAR MY CRY
(Mary Magdalene)

O God hear my cry,
for my loss is more than I can bear;
I am surrounded by darkness,
and I do not know myself.

In the hours before the dawn I will arise,
while it is still dark.
Through the streets of the city, and in the cold garden,
among those who have disappeared,
and at the site of sudden death,
at the place of my abandonment,
and deep in my heart's anger, I will search you out.

In the speechless places of my soul,
and in that which I most fear, I will seek you;
through the strange landscape of my grief
I will return to the darkness
as to my mother's womb.

I shall not fear wounding,
nor shall I be appalled by violent men;
for the grave is naked before God,
the pain of death has no covering.

I sought you early, my beloved,
but you had turned and gone.
I came while it was still dark;
I put my hand to the rock.
I looked for touch, and behold, terror;
for grief, and behold, annihilation.

Horror engulfed me,
and I did not hear your voice;
I was clothed with my tears,
your face was hidden from me.
Then was I compelled by your presence,
and my heart turned within me.
Like the sudden rain upon the grass
and like the sunlight
my God is come to me;
as the footfall of a child who was lost,
as the rhythm of an unremembered song.

Your coming is like freedom to the prisoner,
like the return of those long captive.
You are the movements of the dance I had forgotten,
you are the face of satisfied desire.

My soul is stirred for you, my beloved,
I cannot contain my heart;
for you have seen my longing,
and your eyes are dark with love.
Your love is stronger than death,

your passion more relentless than the grave.
You will but speak the word,
and I shall be healed;
though your touch is the touch of a stranger,
yet is your voice my home.

John 20.1–18
Song of Songs 5.2–8

Poems

THAT NIGHT WE GATHERED

That night we gathered for the birth, as women
have always done – as women
have never done till now;
and in an ordinary room,
warm, exposed, and intimate as childbed,
we spoke about our bodies and our blood,
waiting for God's delivery:
silence, gesture, and speech
announcing, with a strange appropriate blend
of mystery and bluntness,
the celebration of the word made flesh
midwived wholly by women.

THEY HAVE TAKEN AWAY MY LORD
(Mary Magdalene)

It was unfinished.
We stayed there, fixed, until the end,
women waiting for the body that we loved;
and then it was unfinished.
There was no time to cherish, cleanse, anoint;
no time to handle him with love,
no farewell.

Since then, my hands have waited,
aching to touch even his deadness,
smoothe oil into bruises that no longer hurt,
offer his silent flesh my finished act of love.

I came early, as the darkness lifted,
to find the grave ripped open and his body gone;
container of my grief smashed, looted,
leaving my hands still empty.

I turned on the man who came:
'They have taken away my Lord – where is his corpse?
Where is the body that is mine to greet?
He is not gone
I am not ready yet, I am not finished –
I cannot let him go
I am not whole.'

And then he spoke, no corpse,
and breathed,
and offered me my name.
My hands rushed to grasp him;
to hold and hug and grip his body close;
to give myself again, to cling to him,
and lose my self in love.
'Don't touch me now.'

I stopped, and waited, my rejected passion
hovering between us like some dying thing.
I, Mary, stood and grieved, and then departed.

I have a gospel to proclaim.

John 20.1–18 *Mary Magdalene at the tomb*

I NEVER MEANT YOU TO ROLL BACK THE STONE
(Women at the tomb)

I never meant you to roll back the stone
before I was ready to ask.
I had not even fingered
the roughness and edge of it,
tested my shoulder against its painful weight,
stood contemplating its massive shadow,
or wept in the half dark for a miracle
I would not have accepted.

How can I want what I wanted
but never believed in?
Despair was at least articulate, unstrange:
I knew what the repeated question was,
endlessly safe from an answer.
Not this open grave,
this violation of my certainty, this
chill ecstasy I can no longer refuse,
this fear I flee from without hope
it will leave me behind;
this large, gratuitous terror
I cannot now seek refuge from
without complete betrayal.

You, beloved,
for whom I stretched my heart with grief,
rudely announce its irrelevance;
arising to my unreadiness
not with a comfortable word,
but to a world appalled.

Mark 16.1–8

IN DARKNESS AND ANXIETY
(after John of the Cross)

In darkness and anxiety
I searched for her continually,
treading again the paths of my confusion,
knowing I know nothing.

In darkness and aridity
I longed for her variety,
absorbed and aching with my neediness,
feeling I know nothing.

In darkness and in emptiness
I pleaded for her tenderness,

fingering the pain of my familiar loss,
fearing to know nothing.

In darkness and in urgency
I courted her insistently,
leaning towards the kisses of her mouth,
yearning to know nothing.

In darkness and obscurity
I waited for her secretly,
learning to hide the face of my desire,
choosing to know nothing.

In darkness and security
she came to me abundantly,
touching the speechless and reluctant part of me
needing to know nothing.

MY GHOSTLY FRIEND
(after The Cloud of Unknowing*)*

My ghostly friend,
when you have finished splitting into fragments
the self that I had just perceived as one;
when you have neatly filtered out my senses,
imagination, feeling, intellectual grasp,
even my insights painfully acquired,
and left me nothing, whole;
when I have once again learned to forget
the knowledge I was not supposed to seek,
and treated with familiar contempt
this homely, blabbering flesh;
agreed to contemplate that pure interior core
I don't believe is there;
then give me back the language of my body:
naked, blind, groping, and intently stirred,
battering like a baby on that cloud,
or playing seriously as a lover
the game of secrecy.

For my body knows the lumpiness of sin
is not the barrier: with lovers,
blemishes are not ashamed to show,
but can be cautiously exposed, forgiven, cherished even
as kindly oddities.
What must be covered is that little private love
that knows itself too much;
so I will practise modesty with God,
letting my body teach me the unknowing
passion itself requires;
and trust my lover also to pretend,
hiding within a shadow that protects me
against annihilation.

RUTH HAD THE STRAIGHTFORWARD PART
(Ruth and Naomi)

Ruth had the straightforward part:
to empty out her past,
turn from her own gods,
give herself without a thought,
fall into the arms of that safe woman,
and ask to be held for ever.
But Naomi, burnt out and battered by God,
with no resources but her brokenness,
took into her body that deep well of need,
touched her with tenderness,
led her into a strange land,
and asked her to let go.

I WANT SO MUCH THIS FREEDOM

I want so much this freedom,
this life not pain-free
but unparalysed;
this movement, chosen
not without struggle
but loosed from self-wounding,
corrupt obedience to an evil law.
This work, uninflicted, whole, exuberant,
I have wanted this so much.

I WANT TO WRESTLE WITH YOU NOW

I want to wrestle with you now   cradle you
follow your words closely   argue fiercely
stand my ground   learn from you
walk close with you
insist on my own path
forget you   never forget you.

I want you to speak to my weaknesses
measure my strength
enfold my heart   dance free
flash fire with me   touch me
love your solitude   turn to me
surrender   never surrender.

I TOO WAS MADE BY TOUCHING

I too was made by touching.
My blurred body
sweet flesh contained,
massaged into birth
and moulded with embraces.
My soul from cherishing
received her definition;
I was articulated first by a caress.

YOU ARE THE TOUCH OF THE SEA

You are the touch of the sea when it is like silk
you are the boulders that embrace the bay
you are the warm clouds holding the sun
the light that spills over them like wine
and the smooth water's sheen.
You are my body's buoyancy
and the deep currents that bear me
you are the silence at my centre
and the stillness of the attentive sky.
You are the arms that hold me
and in your body's depths I am contained.

TO FIND MYSELF EXPOSED

To find myself exposed
where even the dark is not safe;
to suffer my timid flesh
to be appalled with longing;
to give up all my words
and unprotect my soul;
to be searched with love,
and scorched with the breath of you;
I cannot so much as finger this fear
for fear of unforgetting.

WITH YOUR WARM HANDS

With your warm hands heal me
in your body know me
to your darkness draw me
at your breast hold me.
For I was homesick,
and you brought me home;
I was alone,
and now I am in touch;
my words were alien to me,
you spoke my mother tongue.

CURIOUSLY SAFE

Curiously safe
I weep unforbidden
finally   not resisting your love
my words unready
my body unguarded
my heart no longer
choosing restraint
I cry unknowing   with the child in me
who   unwept till now
would not be held.

AND YOU HELD ME

and you held me and there were no words
and there was no time and you held me
and there was only wanting and
being held and being filled with wanting
and I was nothing but letting go
and being held
and there were no words and there
needed to be no words
and there was no terror   only stillness
and I was wanting nothing and
it was fullness and it was like aching for God
and it was touch and warmth and
darkness and no time and no words and we flowed
and I flowed and I was not empty
and I was given up to the dark and
in the darkness   I was not lost
and the wanting was like fullness and I could
hardly hold it and I was held and
you were dark and warm and without time and
without words and you held me

THE BODIES OF GROWNUPS

The bodies of grownups
come with stretchmarks and scars,
faces that have been lived in,
relaxed breasts and bellies,
backs that give trouble,
and well-worn feet:
flesh that is particular,
and obviously mortal.
They also come
with bruises on their heart,
wounds they can't forget,
and each of them
a company of lovers in their soul
who will not return
and cannot be erased.
And yet I think there is a flood of beauty
beyond the smoothness of youth;
and my heart aches for that grace of longing
that flows through bodies
no longer straining to be innocent,
but yearning for redemption.

Thy Kingdom Come

Reflections on the Lord's Prayer

THE LORD'S PRAYER – A TRANSLATION

Abba our God,
whom the heavens disclose,
may your name be held holy,
your authority come.
May your longing be fulfilled
as in heaven, so on earth.
Give us today
the bread of tomorrow,
and cancel our debts
as we have already
forgiven our debtors.
Do not draw us in
to sinful enticement,
but set us free
from the grip of evil;
for authority and power and glory
are yours alone, for ever,
Amen.

LORD, LORD!

We want to worship you, the one true God.
  But there are several other realities
  we find it necessary to live our lives by.
Give us the purity of heart that truly seeks you,
and will not be deflected or deceived
by other claims on our allegiance.

We pray 'Thy Kingdom Come'.
  But we are not expecting it just yet.
Give us your urgent longing,
which is restless until the hungry shall be filled,
tears wiped away,
and the poor shall hear good news at last.

We call you 'Lord, Lord!'
But we find it hard to think about power
without becoming curiously vague.
Give us the truthfulness
to mean what we say and sing,
to face the institutions that work in our self-interest;
to be prepared to give up
all our advantages
save that of knowing
that the kingdom, the power and the glory are yours
and yours alone,
now and for ever.
Amen.

MAY YOUR NAME BE HOLY

Merciful God,
as the company of those you have
ransomed and redeemed,
we come together in your name
to stand up for life
against every form of slavery.

Against the powerful who use your name
for their own purposes
we come together to make your name holy.

May your name be holy
in this time of worship
and in the places where our worship will lead
   us in this week.

May your name be holy
in the songs and prayers we share together
and in our words and actions after we part.

May your name be holy
among those we know well
and those we have never met;
among all who long, with us,
for your kingdom to come.

THE BREAD OF TOMORROW

A prayer of approach

We're here because we're hungry
for all that God offers:
for acceptance, for challenge,
for a place and a people
who want to be with us,
who want to feast with us
whoever we are, and whatever we bring.
Give us today our daily bread:
All: Give us today the bread of tomorrow.

We're here because we're hungry
for all that God offers:
for a taste of the truth –
that all is not hopeless,
that we are not helpless,
that the powers of this world
the rules of the market
will yield to God's rule.
Give us today our daily bread:
All: Give us today the bread of tomorrow.

FORGIVE US OUR DEBTS

Reflection on the Lord's Prayer

O God to whom we owe
more than we can count,
in our desire to control
all that will come to be,
we hold your other children
in the grip of debt
which they cannot repay;
and make them suffer now
the poverty we dread.
Do not hold us to our debts,
but unchain our fear,
that we may release others

into an open future
of unbounded hope
through Jesus Christ our Saviour.
Amen.

DELIVER US FROM EVIL

Reflection on the Lord's Prayer

God our redeemer,
you have promised
liberation for our world:
remission of debts,
forgiveness of sins.
Deliver us, body, mind and spirit
from the grip of all that is evil;
and may we who claim the blessing of release
have courage to live by it,
in the name of him who died to set us free,
Jesus Christ our Lord.
Amen.

YOURS IS THE KINGDOM

Let us proclaim our commitment to live,
not under the rule of evil,
but under the reign of God.

We will not live under the rule of evil
where some children die
for lack of proper food.
We will live by your kingdom,
where you are preparing on this earth
a feast for all the poor.
For yours is the kingdom,
the power and the glory.

We will not live under the rule of evil
where some are trapped by debt
in desperate poverty.
We will live by your kingdom,

where prisoners lose their chains
and those who are paralysed walk free.
For yours is the kingdom,
the power and the glory.

We will not live under the rule of evil
which lays heavy burdens
on those who cannot bear them
and lifts not a finger to help.
We will live by your kingdom
where all who find release
will long for others to be free.
For yours is the kingdom,
the power and the glory,
for ever and ever. Amen.

YOUR KINGDOM COME

It's that visit you never made;
the seeds you forgot about
that took over the garden;
the child you ignored;
the dough you set aside;
the treasure you trod on
digging for something else;
the tapwater that was left
when the wine ran out.
It's the overgrown field
where you can't tell weeds from wheat;
it's that antique you missed
lying dusty among the junk;
the invite you turned down,
the party where you came too late,
or didn't dress up for.

Hurry, search the city streets
and scour the country lanes –
compel them to come in;
I want my house full!

Scatter the seed
bake the bread
pour the wine
fill the house
bring the children
and come to the party.

The invitation can't wait
till the guests are readier
or the task easier.
The matter is urgent
the feast is ready
and the time is now.

*Hurry, search the city streets
and scour the country lanes –
compel them to come in;
I want my house full!*

Scatter the seed
bake the bread
pour the wine
fill the house
bring the children
and come to the party.

The invitation can't wait
till the world is fairer,
or the time is riper.
The matter is urgent
the feast is ready
and the time is now.

*Hurry, search the city streets
and scour the country lanes –
compel them to come in;
I want my house full!*

Scatter the seed
bake the bread
pour the wine
fill the house
bring the children
and come to the party.

Luke 14.12–24

Harvest Prayers

FEAST OF LIFE

Prayer of adoration
Harvest, Communion

Praise to our God,
our help in ages past,
who has nourished us, body and spirit,
and raised up in every generation
saints and workers for justice
who gave us the ground we stand on
and planted the seeds of change.

Praise to our God,
our hope for years to come,
who makes us dream generous dreams
of a harvest shared,
of sufferings ended,
of the time when all shall be included
in one great feast of life.

Praise to our God
who daily offers us
this present moment
to renounce despair,
to leave behind our fear,
and choose that community of freedom
where those who are poor come first,
but all who kneel and open their hands
shall be unfailingly fed.

HARVEST INTERCESSIONS

O God our creator,
whose good earth is entrusted
to our care and delight and tenderness,
we pray:

For all who are in captivity to debt,
whose lives are cramped with fear
from which there is no turning
except through abundant harvest.

May those who sow in tears
Reap with shouts of joy.

For all who depend on the earth
for their daily food and fuel
whose forests are destroyed
for the profits of a few.

May those who sow in tears
Reap with shouts of joy.

For all who labour in poverty,
who are oppressed by unjust laws,
who are banned for speaking the truth,
who long for a harvest of justice.

May those who sow in tears
Reap with shouts of joy.

For all who are in captivity
to greed and waste and boredom,
whose harvest joy is choked
with things they do not need.

May those who sow in tears
Reap with shouts of joy.

Turn us again from our captivity
and restore our vision,
that our mouth may be filled with laughter
and our tongue with singing.

Psalm 126

PRAYER OF THANKSGIVING

O Eternal Wisdom,
who laid the foundations of the earth,
and breathed life into every creature,
creating us in our variety
to cherish your world and seek your face:
we praise you and give you thanks
for your abundant love towards this earth,
violated with our injustice,
and polluted by our sin;
because you took upon you our unprotected flesh,
and entered our struggle,
that you might deliver all creation
from its bondage to oppression and decay.

Therefore, with those whose voice is silenced,
with those who call for freedom,
those whose harvest celebration
sings through hardship and labour and love;
and crying with them for that new creation
when the morning stars shall sing together,
and all the children of God shout for joy,
we praise you, saying

**Holy, holy, holy,
all-creative God,
heaven and earth are full of your glory.
Hosanna in the highest.**

THE WORK OF YOUR HANDS

Harvest prayer

O God, you have created us,
hands and mind and heart,
to find our satisfaction in hard and skilful work,
and to delight in sharing its harvest.
With all who labour

we offer ourselves
to be the work of your hands
in making a world
where no one will be exhausted
by toil that is fruitless;
but all may enjoy to the full
what their own hands have produced.
In the name of Christ, **Amen.**

Reflections on the Beatitudes

THE BEATITUDES – A PARAPHRASE

Blessed are those whose spirit has been shaped by poverty;
for theirs is the kingdom of heaven.

Blessed are those who are sick at heart to see power abused;
for they shall be invited to the feast.

Blessed are those who are not arrogant;
for they shall inherit the earth.

Blessed are those who are desperate for justice;
for they shall eat and drink their fill.

Blessed are the compassionate;
for they shall have compassion shown to them when they
    need it.

Blessed are those who refuse to be corrupted;
for they shall not be afraid to come face to face with God.

Blessed are those who take action to bring about peace;
for they shall truly be called God's own.

Blessed are those who carry wounds suffered in the struggle
    for justice;
for theirs is the kingdom of heaven.

Matthew 5.1–12

THEY SHALL BE SATISFIED

Reflection on the Beatitudes

O God,
you have made us creatures of this earth,
hungry and thirsty and needy,
that you might satisfy all our longings
with your abundant love.
Satisfy the hunger of our bodies
    for food and shelter, health and human touch.
Satisfy the hunger of our spirits
    for dignity and freedom
    in giving and receiving.
Satisfy the hunger of our minds
    to understand our world,
    the reasons for its pain,
    the ways we are connected to each other.
Satisfy the hunger of our hearts
    that all who share this loving earth with us
    shall share our satisfaction.
And satisfy the hunger of our hands
    to help you make it so
through Jesus Christ.
Amen.

Eucharist

APPROACH

The vision of God

Prayer of approach and confession
Trinity Sunday

Lord of all holiness,
when we approach your glory,
we are conscious of our guilt,
conscious of our people's guilt
in a world where so many live in hardship.
We feel that we are lost,
helpless to act or change.
You bring us the offer of hope,
but we are afraid of it.
You bring us the words of life,
but our words are full of despair;
our lips are unclean.
Touch our lips with your holy fire,
cleanse us and take away our guilt.
Make our hearts ready to say:
'Here am I, Lord, send me.'

Isaiah 6.1–8

Prayer of approach

O God,
nothing about our bodily life
is alien to you.
By taking human flesh,
its tenderness, its limits,
you have shown your limitless love for us.

So we are not afraid
to bring our bodies
into your presence,
into each other's company.

We did not stay at home;
we did not choose to remain alone,
but we have brought our own immediate lives,
our private burdens,
all that is weighing on us now, at this time,
all that gives us delight,
into this common life.
We give thanks for our bodies;
they make us human
they give us sympathy
for other human bodies.
And so we choose to grasp
not only our own pain,
not only the demands and pleasures
of our particular place,
but the suffering and hope of those
from whom the world divides us.

We know we are fragile,
we cannot carry such awareness
without your solid love to bear the weight.
But teach us to long, with you,
for a world where,
not just in our own lives
but in all lives,
the burden of hunger is lifted
and evil holds no grip.

Let us pray in the words that Jesus taught us:
Lord's Prayer

Can these bones live?

O God, the source of our common life,
when we are dry and scattered,
when we are divided and alone,
we long for connection, we long for community.
Breath of God, breathe on us.

With those we live beside,
who are often strange to us,
whom we may be afraid to approach,
yet who have riches of friendship to share,
we long for connection, we long for community.
Breath of God, breathe on us.

With those we have only heard of,
who see with different eyes,
whose struggles we try to imagine,
whose fierce joy we wish we could grasp,
we long for connection, we long for community.
Breath of God, breathe on us.

With those we shall never know,
but whose lives are linked with ours,
whose shared ground we stand on,
and whose common air we breathe,
we long for connection, we long for community.
Breath of God, breathe on us.

When we are dry and scattered,
when we are divided and alone,
when we are cut off from the source of our life,
open our graves, O God,
that all your people
may be free to breathe, strong to move,
and joyful to stand together
to celebrate your name. **Amen.**

'The breath came into them, and they lived, and stood
on their feet, a vast multitude.'
Ezekiel 37.1–14

CONFESSION

O God, you have invited us to come to you
and lay our burdens down.
We confess our part in the world's sin:
we lay before you
the sufferings we see on the news,
the heavy loads that we impose
whether we know it or not
that others have to carry.
Remembering them is painful to us

The burden of them is intolerable.

We lay before you
the widening gap between rich and poor,
the economic policies that promote selfishness
and destroy community spirit
here and around the world.
Remembering them is painful to us

The burden of them is intolerable.

We lay before you
the activities of global bodies
that end up hurting the poorest
and leaving them destitute;
the double standards that are applied
to protect the rich and expose the poor.
Remembering them is painful to us

The burden of them is intolerable.

We lay before you our heaviest burdens:
our refusal to repent,
our desire to forget,
our exhausting efforts to believe
that we are separate from this sin, these sufferings.
Remembering them is painful to us

The burden of them is intolerable.

INTERCESSION

Weep not for me

Reflection for Good Friday

Let us pray for women in our world who have cause to weep.
To women who grieve for the future of children
they cannot feed or educate or clothe,
Jesus says:

Men: Weep not for me
Women: but weep for yourselves and for your children.

To women who have to watch their children die
from disease, hunger or violence,
Jesus says:

Men: Weep not for me
Women: but weep for yourselves and for your children.

To women whose children have disappeared, or are in exile;
or who are separated from their children because of their
  own detention,
Jesus says:

Men: Weep not for me
Women: but weep for yourselves and for your children.

To women whose bodies and minds are violated
by sexual attack, exploitation, or degrading images,
Jesus says:

Men: Weep not for me
Women: but weep for yourselves and for your children.

To women whose work is discounted, and whose voice is
  unvalued,
Jesus says:

Men: Weep not for me
Women: but weep for yourselves and for your children.

'A great number of people followed him, and among them
were women who were beating their breasts and wailing for him.'
Luke 23.27–31

OFFERTORY

Hands like these

O God, your feast is prepared by hands like these.
Through your goodness we have this bread to offer
through your goodness we have our hands to offer
and our homes, our hearts, our hospitality.
You take our hands,
skilled or clumsy, strong or aching,
smooth-skinned or knobbly or tough.
And you teach us with them
to touch with respect
the hands we can reach
the hands we can't reach
invisible hands
that work for their lives
that work for our lives.
You take our homes,
everyday places
of freedom and selfishness,
of beauty and chaos and love,
and ask us to open them
not just to our friends,
our family and relations,
the neighbours we have to live with
or the people we want to impress,
but to those we don't know
and can't quite imagine –
to open our homes
and fill them with laughter
as your house is full.
You take our lives,

ordinary as wheat or cornmeal,
daily as bread,
our stumbling generosity,
our simple actions,
and you find them good enough
to open the door to your kingdom.

Take our hands

Offertory prayer

Living God,
take our hands,
take our lives,
ordinary as wheat or cornmeal,
daily as bread –
our stumbling generosity,
our simple actions,
and find them good enough
to help prepare the feast
for all your people.
Amen.

Offering our bodies

An offertory prayer, before Communion

We bring you our bodies:
embarrassed, unfit, uncomforted,
bruised by neglect, or overworked and tense.
We bring you our bodies:
tender and accurate,
the place where the world touches us,
full of the knowledge of pleasure,
and understanding pain.

O Christ, who shared our human flesh,
make us one body with you.

We bring you the bodies of others across the world,
different from ours, strange to us, attractive,
making us fearful or curious or ashamed.
We bring you the bodies of others, not separate from ours,
but aching together if one person suffers;
rejoicing together when one person sings.

O Christ, who shared our human flesh,
make us one body with you.

We bring you your body,
sharing our life and growth,
knowing our pleasure,
not shrinking from our love,
our sickness, fear and pain.
We bring you your body,
strong in the knowledge of death,
risen with the power of love,
declaring to every fragile human body
that we are not alone.

O Christ, who shared our human flesh,
make us one body with you.

COMMITMENT

Enlarging our hearts

O God who gave us life to cherish and enjoy,
and made us capable, in its service,
of costly love and powerful commitment:
help us to choose life in all its abundance,
not only for ourselves and for our children,
but for all our struggling world,
for whom you were content to lay down your life
in Jesus Christ our Lord.
Amen.

Changing the world

O God, you promise a world
where those who now weep shall laugh;
those who are hungry shall feast;
those who are poor now, and excluded,
shall have your kingdom for their own.
I want this world too.
I renounce despair.
I will act for change.
I choose to be included
in your great feast of life.

> 'Faith by itself, if it has no works, is dead.'
> James 2.14–17

The easy yoke

Prayer of commitment

O Christ,
you have offered us your easy yoke,
the yoke of love.
It is easier to bear than remaining alone,
easier than believing we can do nothing,
easier than keeping the world out,
and trying to close our hearts.
So, yoke us together with earth's poorest people,
that we may weep with their pain,
rejoice in their hope
be their companions in the struggle,
and find our own salvation
as members of your body,
through your holy name, **Amen.**

> 'Take my yoke upon you, and learn from me; for I am gentle and
> humble in heart, and you will find rest for your souls.'
> Matthew 11.29

We give you back our lives

*Prayer of commitment
suitable for the New Year*

O God who gave us life,
and in whose arms we die,
you know us as we are,
understand what we have been,
and see what we shall become.
We give you back our lives
that you may make them new:
generous, committed to hope,
and fearless to do your will;
that your whole creation
may live to praise your name
now and for ever. **Amen.**

BLESSING

Beauty instead of ashes

*A blessing for Ash Wednesday or in
time of grief*

May the God who binds up the broken-hearted,
who proclaims freedom to the captive
and promises justice
to all who mourn its loss,
bless you with beauty instead of ashes,
the oil of gladness in place of grief,
and instead of your spirit of despair,
a garment of unending praise;
through Jesus Christ our Lord, **Amen.**

Isaiah 60.1–3

Short Prayers and Reflections

AT HOME WITH YOU
A grace, especially in times of transition

O Lord our God,
our help in ages past
our refuge in time of fear:
bless to us today
the food on our table
and the love in our hearts;
that wherever life takes us,
we may be at home with you.

CHILD LABOURERS

Below the level of my sight,
I find the lowly tasks are done
not just by those who are poor,
but by the children –
responsible, serious,
shouldering the adult burden
before they are fully grown.
God give them time to play,
and live and dream,
as I am free to do.

CHILDREN OF CONFLICT

O God, deliver our world
from the recurring conflicts
that close borders,
close schools,
close minds,
and shut off the future.
Give the children freedom

to learn from their heritage,
read their own language,
and take pride in their people.

> 'Unless you change and become like children, you will never enter
> the kingdom of heaven.'
> Matthew 18.1–5

CHRISTMAS PRAYER
For children born in poverty or danger

Christ our God,
you too were born a child
not free into our world:
subject to poverty,
harassment by foreign powers,
and dangers to your health.
In your name
let us cry freedom for your children
now, at this time,
and through all generations.

> 'They shall not labour in vain, or bear children for calamity.'
> Isaiah 65.17–23

DO YOU WANT TO BE HEALED?
For broken or occupied communities

Yes, we want to be healed:
as the dry well longs for water,
as the exile for her home;
as the father wants his children,
and the broken house
demands its people back.
Yes, we want to be healed:
as those who live in fear of the enemy
wish they could breathe safe;
as the fence that divided the village
prefers to be torn down;

as children who dream bad dreams
need an unbroken night;
as those who have long been paralysed
now choose to move.

John 5.6

FAIR TRADE
A consumer's prayer

God of the just weight
and the fair measure,
let me remember the hands
that harvested my food, my drink,
not only in my prayers
but in the marketplace.
Let me not seek a bargain
that leaves another hungry.

'You shall not withhold the wages of poor and needy labourers.'
Deuteronomy 24.15

HONOUR AND RESPECT
For those who are given no respect

When honour or respect
are not daily what greets me;
when my work is unvalued,
my needs dismissed,
or my voice unheard,
teach me my dignity.
For with you, O Lord, I have confidence,
and in your presence
I shall never be put to shame.

'The Lord is the stronghold of my life; of whom shall I be afraid?'
Psalm 27.1

LIVING WITH LOSS OR CALAMITY

O compassionate Lord,
I would prefer power over the storm,
a secure home,
a life protected from the winds.
But help me to live with storms,
shelter with friends,
see my plans broken,
but not my life;
rebuild again and again from the earth.

LOSS AND HOPE
For those who have been forcibly made homeless

O God, you bring hope out of emptiness
energy out of fear,
new life out of grief and loss.
Comfort all who have lost their homes
through persecution, war, exile,
or deliberate destruction.
Give them security, a place to live,
and neighbours they trust
to be, with them,
a new sign of peace to the world. **Amen.**

NOTHING IS WASTED
Reflections on what we call rubbish

O God,
with whom nothing is lost, nothing is wasted,
we thank you for the miracle of compost –
our daily leavings, what we throw away,
able, with time and care,
to fertilize the earth.
Take what we regard as useless in our lives,
failure, pain or poverty,

and transform them through your power
to become a rich source of growth.

Mark 4. 30–32

THE INVISIBLE ONES
For those who keep our world clean

Christ our Lord,
who took a towel, bent down,
and wiped the feet of your friends,
wash our hearts also.
Remember the invisible ones
who keep our world clean:
clothes, homes, offices, streets.
May we not despise this work
which serves our self-respect,
nor keep people trapped in poverty
doing our dirty work.

'The greatest among you will be your servant.'
Matthew 23.11–12

THE POWER TO WAIT
*For asylum-seekers, prisoners and anyone who has to wait on
the decisions of others*

Lord of compassion,
it is so hard to feel useless,
to be unable to escape from difficulties,
to be dependent on the will of others,
to have no control.
When there is nothing I can do
to decide the future,
give me the power to wait:
to wait without anger,
to wait without tiring of my life.

'The Son of Man has nowhere to lay his head.'
Matthew 8.20

TO NAME WHAT IS EVIL
*In time of war, genocide, torture or the violation of human
rights*

O God,
we hear and hear, and do not understand.
we see and see, but do not perceive.
Sharpen our memory,
unlock our grief,
teach us to name what is evil
and refuse it:
even when it seems normal
even when it seems necessary
even when it is commanded by religion;
then, now, always. **Amen.**

'Breathe into these slain, that they may live.'
Ezekiel 37.9

TRUTH AND RECONCILIATION
When forgiveness is hard

Jesus our Saviour,
your heart was broken
by the world's agony;
you carried the pain
we make each other bear.
remember those who carry
the difficult work of peace,
bearing the cost of memory,
seeking detailed justice,
facing day by day
the hard recurring choice
whether to ask forgiveness,
whether to forgive.

'If you . . . had only recognized on this day the things that make
for peace!'
Luke 19:41–42

VIA DOLOROSA
Visiting Jerusalem

Jesus our brother,
as we dare to follow
in the steps you trod,
be our companion on the way.
May our eyes see
not only the stones that saw you
but the people who walk with you now;
may our feet tread
not only the path of your pain
but the streets of a living city;
may our prayers embrace
not only the memory of your presence
but the flesh and blood who jostle us today.
Bless us, with them, and make us long
to do justice, to love mercy,
and to walk humbly with our God.
Amen.

WHEN I COME TO DIE
Prayer for the dying, and when preparing for death

When I come to die,
give me companions:
cheerful, practical,
able to walk the edge with me
and look me in the eye.
Until that time,
grant me to use fully
each day, each hour,
open-hearted, knowing your love,
savouring my life.

> 'I was sick and you took care of me.'
> Matthew 25.31–45

WOMEN AND WAR

So many women
across the ages
have looked on horror,
seen their men slain,
wept until they have no more tears,
and then had to live.
God give them again
the wish to embrace life;
may they turn to each other and be made strong,
that death may have no more dominion.

'Many women were also there, looking on from a distance.'
Matthew 27.55–56

ALL SAINTS

For all the saints
  who went before us,
  who have spoken to our hearts
  and touched us with your fire,
  we praise you, O God.

For all the saints
  who live beside us,
  whose weaknesses and strengths
  are woven with our own,
  we praise you, O God.

For all the saints
  who live beyond us,
  who challenge us,
  to change the world with them,
  we praise you, O God.

Notes on Copyright

Copyright is shared between Christian Aid and Janet Morley for the following:

From *Dear Life – Praying Through the Year with Christian Aid*, ed. Janet Morley, Hannah Ward and Jennifer Wild, Christian Aid, 1998:

Child labourers – 'Below the level of my sight' p. 18
Children of conflict – 'O God, deliver our world' p. 22
At home with you – 'O Lord our God' p. 30
Women and war – 'So many women' p. 45
Truth and reconciliation – 'Jesus our Saviour' p. 48
Honour and respect – 'When honour or respect' p. 50
Changing the world – 'O God, you promise a world' p. 64
Nothing is wasted – 'O God, with whom nothing is lost' p. 70
The invisible ones – 'Christ our Lord, who took a towel' p. 89
Living with loss or calamity – 'O compassionate Lord' p. 98
The power to wait – 'Lord of compassion' p. 102
Fair trade – 'God of the just weight' p. 115
When I come to die – 'When I come to die' p. 128
Christmas prayer – 'Christ our God' p. 135

From *Companions of God – Praying for Peace in the Holy Land*, ed. Janet Morley, Christian Aid, 1994:

Via dolorosa – 'Jesus our brother' p. 2
Loss and hope – 'O God, you bring hope out of emptiness' p. 14
To name what is evil – 'O God, we hear and hear' p. 23
Do you want to be healed? – 'Yes, we want to be healed' p. 28
Joy beyond measure – 'You have kept the good wine' p. 55 (adapted)

From Christian Aid Week Order of Service 1990, *The World Is Our Community*:

Can these bones live? – 'O God, the source of our common life'

From Christian Aid Week Order of Service 1994, *Invitation to Life*:

Take our hands – 'Living God, take our hands' *(prayer card)*
The bread of tomorrow – 'We're here because we're hungry'
Hands like these – 'O God, your feast is prepared'
Your kingdom come – 'Hurry, search the city streets' *(new material added to beginning)*

From Christian Aid Week Order of Service 1995, *The Life of the Body*:

Prayer of approach – 'O God, nothing about our bodily life is alien to you'
Confession – 'O God, you have invited us'
The easy yoke – 'O Christ, you have offered us your easy yoke'
The burden of love – O God, you took upon you'
Offering our bodies – 'We bring you our bodies' *(Worship Leaders' Guide)*

From Christian Aid Week Order of Service 1998, *Live in Hope*:

The vision of God – 'Lord of all holiness'
Most holy and most humble – 'Mighty God' *(Eucharistic propers)*
Forgive us our debts – 'O God, to whom we owe' *(Worship Leaders' Guide)*

From Christian Aid Week Order of Service 1999, *Life or Debt:*
May your name be holy – 'Merciful God, as the company'
Deliver us from evil – 'God our redeemer'
Yours is the kingdom – 'Let us proclaim our commitment to live'

From Christian Aid autumn anthology 1989, *Till All Creation Sings:*
The Lord's Prayer – a translation – 'Abba our God'
Harvest intercessions – 'O God our creator'
Prayer of thanksgiving – 'O Eternal Wisdom'

From Christian Aid harvest worship 1990, *Tell Out My Soul:*
Tell out my soul – 'O God, whose word is fruitless'

From Christian Aid harvest anthology 1991, *They Shall Not Plant and Another Eat:*
The work of your hands – 'O God, you have created us'

From Christian Aid harvest anthology 1992, *They Shall Be Satisfied:*
They shall be satisfied – 'O God, you have made us creatures of this earth'

From Christian Aid harvest material, *Feast for Life:*
Feast of life – 'Praise to our God, our help in ages past'
Beauty instead of ashes – 'May the God who binds up the broken-hearted'
The Beatitudes – a paraphrase – 'Blessed are those whose spirit has been shaped'

From Christian Aid summer festival 1990, *A Pilgrimage of Prayer:*
Weep not for me – 'Let us pray for women in our world'

From Christian Aid Advent Candle Ceremony 1989, *God With Us:*
God of the poor – 'God of the poor'

From Christian Aid Millennium pack 1999, *New Start:*
We give you back our lives – 'O God who gave us life'

From Christian Aid and the United Reformed Church pack, *Commitment for Life:*
Enlarging our hearts – 'O God who gave us life to cherish and enjoy'

From *Bread of Tomorrow*, ed. Janet Morley, Christian Aid and SPCK, 1992:
All saints – 'For all the saints'

From *Who Runs the World?* – ideas for worship leaders, Christian Aid, 1994:
Lord, Lord! – 'We want to worship you'

CPSIA information can be obtained
at www.ICGtesting.com
Printed in the USA
LVHW081921280720
661504LV00012B/52